GOD

does not . . .

GOD

does not . . .

**entertain,
play "matchmaker,"
hurry, demand blood,
cure every illness**

d. brent laytham, editor

BrazosPress

a division of Baker Publishing Group
Grand Rapids, Michigan

$I. Brazos ⅔₉ 17.99

Published by Brazos Press
a division of Baker Publishing Group
P.O. Box 6287, Grand Rapids, MI 49516-6287
www.brazospress.com

Printed in the United States of America

Library of Congress Cataloging-in-Publication Data
God does not— : entertain, play matchmaker, hurry, demand blood, cure every illness / D. Brent Laytham, editor.
    p.   cm.
  Includes bibliographical references.
  ISBN 978-1-58743-229-3 (pbk.)
  1. God (Christianity) I. Laytham, D. Brent.
  BT103.G6188 2009
  231—dc22
                                                                2008041843

green press INITIATIVE

Contents

Acknowledgments

In one sense, this book owes its genesis to the success of *God Is Not* (Brazos, 2004), a similar collection of essays devoted to culturally critical theology. I am thankful that Rodney Clapp and Brazos Press were willing to hazard another anthology of diatribes against the cultural captivity of American Christianity. I thank Rebecca Cooper for beginning this editorial process and Lisa Ann Cockrel for the lion's share of work in seeing it through to publication.

In another sense, this book owes its existence to the various authors' doctoral training at Duke. Though we represent different disciplines, matriculated in different years, and have five different doctoral advisors between us, we nonetheless share a common commitment to the truth of the gospel and the centrality of the church. In that sense, this book is a work of friendship in the faith, hope, and love of God.

Yet Dan Bell remains the compelling force who pushed me forward with the design and implementation of the project. I am grateful for his encouragement and helpfulness with this book, as well as for his great enduring friendship. I thank my remaining coauthors not only for their contributions here, but for the greater friendship this shared work represents. Rodney

Clapp, Debra Dean Murphy, Steve Long, Joel Shuman, and Byron Stuhlman read portions of the book in draft form and offered indispensable assistance. My student assistants Ingrid Johnson and Mike Langer helped with some of the more tedious dimensions of this effort.

INTRODUCTION

God Does All Things Well

D. Brent Laytham

God Does What?

"God helped me shoot gunman" is the headline in one news report of a tragic shooting in a Colorado Springs megachurch.[1] "Security guard who stopped shooter credits God" headlines the CNN story on its website.[2] Many readers will remember the news reports about the murderous rampage of Matthew Murray on December 10, 2007. What gave this horrible story an intriguing twist, and thus guaranteed it even more news coverage than usual, was that security guard Jeanne Assam repeatedly implicated God in her shooting of Murray. Assam told a news conference: "I was weak, and where I was weak, God made me strong"; "He filled me and he guided me and protected me and many other people. And I'm honored that God chose me."[3]

The incident was horrible and senseless. No one can regret that Murray was stopped long before he fired very many of the thousand bullets he was carrying. But does either that relatively less tragic outcome or Assam's feeling of divine aid convince us that God, so to speak, "took out" Matthew Murray? Should we conceive God's actions in the world along the lines of Divine Sniper? I hope not, but deciding the matter will require both hard theological work on the question of what God does and does not do and imaginative discernment of our present situation. That is the kind of work and discernment this book is intended to foster.

God Does Not!

God Does Not is written by authors convinced that God acts like Jesus of Nazareth. Indeed, we believe God acts like Jesus because Jesus is, quite simply, God in action. Echoing the crowd's response to one of Jesus's healings, we believe that *God does all things well* (see Mark 7:31–37). That is easy enough to see when a man who cannot hear or speak is healed, but a good bit harder to fathom when Jesus is betrayed and condemned and mocked and flogged and crucified. Then God apparently does nothing at all—at least nothing until a third-day resurrection. Yet there it is: the template for divine action in the world is crucifixion—resurrection. So we write with a common conviction that God's will for and way with the world are most fully revealed in the life, death, and resurrection of Jesus Christ. Of course, there are plenty of other visions of what God is up to, but we believe that none of them gets to the heart of the matter like Christ crucified and risen.

Saying that doesn't make the problem of competing visions of divine activity go away; it only locates the lens we will use to discern what God really does or does not do. Take, for example, the question, "Does God make people sick?" Some Christians imagine that God distributes illness—at least diseases like AIDS—as a form of punishment for sin. The logic is this: "If you get sick, God did it because you deserve it." We imagine otherwise, and not only because Jesus refuses that kind of quid pro quo in his assessment of illness (John 9:1–7). More fundamentally, in Jesus's passion we see God revealed not as an afflicter, but rather as the bearer of our griefs and afflictions (Isaiah 53). The contrast between God's giving and God's bearing illness is stark. But adjudicating between them cannot be settled by empirical investigation, or by logic, or even by appeal to scripture, since there is at least some biblical material to support each side (for example, 2 Sam. 12:15). In the end, an act of faithful imagination is required—one that grasps the pattern of God's action in Jesus Christ and then discerns semblances of it in the rough-and-tumble of daily life.

That kind of imaginative discernment of what God is doing in the world is the point of *God Does Not*. It is a work of culturally critical Christian theology that rebuts contemporary distortions of what God is doing in the world. Obviously, some distortions hardly need critique and rebuttal. Contrary to the implication of certain end-zone rituals, God does not distribute touchdowns to his favorite players. (Two of us suspect that this is because God is actually more of a college basketball fan.) Contrary to the claims of some Christians, God does not award the best parking spots to fervent pray-ers; indeed, God does not even work as a parking valet. Certainly, such distortions trivialize God, but our best response is probably just to laugh at them and go on.

There are dozens of other distortions of what God does in the world that seem like plausible expressions of Christian faith. In this book we examine five of them: the notions that God does matchmaking, speaks through popular entertainments, demands blood sacrifice, practices medicine, and works too slowly. These ideas of what God does will require more than derisive laughter or withering silence.

Why? First, because they begin with some grain of theological truth: God does care about marriage (Genesis 2), can communicate even through an ass (Numbers 22), will finally heal us, and so on. Yet that initial truth gets misshapen by false claims about God's purpose and character, often rooted in a failure to locate the center of God's activity in Jesus Christ. A further distorting effect arises from our cultural context, where deep longings and shallow practices now fund our imaginations more frequently and more powerfully than the Christian story and its practices. So it will take careful work to analyze the cultural trends and theological misperceptions that make each distortion seem so natural. Only then will we be in a position to see how a plausible claim like "God does demand blood" fails to measure up to the pattern of God's action in Jesus Christ.

A more extensive engagement is required, secondly, because the distortions we identify are held by committed Christians. We certainly do not intend for our arguments here to demean anyone's faith. Yet that cannot settle the matter of whether these disputed claims are genuinely Christian, for even committed Christians are capable of shoddy thinking about God. And to misstate what God is doing is usually also to mistake what God wants us to do. So our thinking about God—whether shoddy or wise—is always implicated in our living. Thus the point of *God Does Not* is less to purify thought than to facilitate living with and for the God who does all things well.

God Does Not . . . What?

I don't intend to settle the question of whether God does or doesn't help us shoot straight when a deranged gunman invades our church building. But that incident and the way people talked about it suggest to me three themes that are intrinsic to most of the chapters of this book. First, there is a strong connection between divine action and happy endings. In the interviews given by Jeanne Assam (and also by her pastor), it is not entirely clear whether they are claiming that "because God acted, things turned out right" or the inverse, that "because things turned out right, we know that God acted." But either way, the danger is that our notion of what a happy ending looks like will owe more to the promises of technology or the fictions of Hollywood than to the

Gospel accounts of Jesus. God does not work happy endings on our terms, but on God's.

Second, the Colorado Springs incident helps us to see the way that violence is woven into our discernments of divine action. I don't mean the way God acts in spite of our sinful propensities to violence, but rather claims that God produces happy endings by doing violence. Whether imagining how God saves sinners, or rids the world of evil, or makes my life come out right, this construal of divine action looks more like our contemporary action heroes than like the suffering Savior who sheathed Peter's sword and refused to call angels into battle (Matt. 26:52–53). God does not work characteristically through violence, but through a love that is relentlessly patient and persuasive.

Finally, the story of the shooting illustrates how often and easily the focus in discerning divine action becomes self-referential. The question being asked and answered is "What is God doing for me?" Of course, God does care for each one of us, and so each Christian is called to offer testimony and thanksgiving for all that God does on his or her behalf. But the logic of faith does not put me or you as the focus of divine action. Faith's center is God in Christ reconciling the whole of creation (Col. 1:20) and redeeming the people of God (Titus 2:14). To put it crassly, God does not work for me or for you either.

In "God Does Not Wear a White Coat—but God Does Heal," Joel Shuman turns our attention to the hopes for a happy ending that we invest in the practice of medicine. Given the powerful successes of modern medicine, and our cultural obsessions with staying young and staving off death, even Christians begin to entrust their hopes for a happy ending to health care. Too easily we reduce God to "little more than a member of the health care team, one who exists primarily to help us live as long and as free from suffering and disability as we possibly can." Of course, God does heal, as Shuman displays in a rich summary of biblical material. But the scriptural focus on divine healing differs significantly from ours.

First, the Bible's vision of health is ecological—oriented toward a health that is communal rather than individualistic. Second, it is evangelical (related to the gospel) in that it sees our present health as "a foreshadowing of the absolute healing that will take place at the consummation of God's redemptive work."

Shuman invites us to shift our focus from limited health care outcomes to God's identity. With Moses at the burning bush and with Jesus in Gethsemane we encounter a God "simultaneously wild and faithful." In Christ's cross we see that God "rules history in the unlikeliest of ways." So we can trust that God will finally heal the whole creation, ourselves included, but in the meantime we cannot expect lives untouched by illness. Christians are called to recognize and live God's healing work in the church, by discerning the proper uses of medicine, by offering the gift of presence in the midst of illness, and by caring hospitality. Rather than put God in a white coat, we are called to be the church, "agents of the wild, faithful God who heals."

Unfortunately, Christians have been far too willing to imagine that God heals the world with violence. Dan Bell helps us to see why in "God Does Not Demand Blood: Beyond Redemptive Violence." Bell points out that the logic of blood sacrifice is not limited to cultures that practiced the sacrifice of lambs or chickens. This ancient notion that violent bloodletting sets things right—indeed, is the only way to set things right—has captured our imagination today as well. So in everything from our response to terrorism to the way we try to "fix" crime, unexpected pregnancies, or our incessant boredom, we assume that violence is the answer. Where we aren't fixing the world by *doing* violence, Bell claims we are trapped by the notion "that sometimes it is redemptive to *suffer* violence."

We cannot dismiss the logic of blood sacrifice out of hand, however, because according to some interpretations of our redemption, that is precisely how God in Christ saves us. The heart of Bell's argument is his explanation of how "Christ's work on the cross is nothing less than the divine refusal of blood sacrifice, as well as any notion that suffering violence is or can be redemptive." He offers a rereading of Anselm's theology in which Christ's death was not appeasement of a wrathful God, but rather God's loving effort to reestablish communion with us alienated creatures. Certainly Christ's cross was violent, but that violence was not God's, and it was not redemptive. Instead, God redeems us by a relentless love that opens for us a way beyond the logic of blood sacrifice, a way that joins us to Christ as participants in his ongoing reconciliation of all creation.

Violence can take other forms, as our next two chapters show. In "God Does Not Hurry," Kelly Johnson helps us to see that hurry is a form of violence that is incompatible with God's patient peaceableness. Given the frenetic pace of daily life and the flat-out velocity of cultural change, hurry has become our common fate. Like everyone else living in this rush toward the next and the new, Christians begin to embody the logic of haste. For example, take the urgency people feel to make Christian faith "relevant" to our rapidly changing culture; this imperative is governed by the sense that our hurry is the only means to keep God savingly connected to the world. God, on the other hand, apparently does not hurry, no matter how much we might wish that God did.

Johnson reveals our addiction at the outset, by noting that Superman is the kind of god we would really like to have—a god who hurries. We want a god like this because of "our sense that we live in a world whose deepest reality is a life-threatening lack of time." In such a world, what else could we do but hurry? And we have the technology to speed us on our way. Curiously, though, the speed of technological change and the logic of technological efficiency have quickly mastered us, leaving us addicted and vulnerable to hurry. God, on the other hand, takes time rather than makes haste. In covenant, God commits to mend the world with patient love. In Jesus we see God's "strange and disturbing patience" fully exemplified. In Jesus we also begin to see how "those who long for God to hurry up and act may not need to sacrifice their passion for justice in order to cultivate a hope that can endure waiting." Indeed, as people of a God who does not hurry, we are given all the time we need to worship and serve God. Johnson explores what this looks like in monastic life and in the L'Arche communities, not to suggest that it is impossible in ordinary life, but precisely to show what it would look like in our families, neighborhoods, and schools. Our patience is no cover for complacency, however; it is instead a resolute commitment "to listen in the unfolding of time for God's music, and to accept the invitation to join our voices to it."

So we find ourselves caught up in a long love story that stretches from the creation of all things to the marriage supper of the Lamb, a tale in which God patiently beckons and woos us toward wholeness. Recognizing the kind of tale we are in can help us avoid yet another distortion—contemporary Christian fantasies of romantic love. In "God Does Not Want to Write Your Love Story," Margaret Kim Peterson and Dwight Peterson offer a compelling rebuttal of the supposedly Christian ideal of a "perfect love story." We don't have to look any further than Jeanne Assam's news conference for evidence that the Petersons' chapter is desperately needed. When asked whether she is married, Assam replied, "I'm not married yet. God's going to find me the perfect man."[4] So yet again we see how our idea of what God does is distorted by a desire for Hollywood happy endings, by self-absorption, and by a propensity for violence. Of course, the violent nature of a perfect Christian love story is not obvious, since it comes bedecked with all the trappings of romance and intends to remedy the pain of loneliness. But as the Petersons show quite convincingly (without ever using the term *violence*), a so-called Christian love story does violence to proper human relationships, to the Christian story, and to our ability to love particular, flesh-and-blood people. "Romance, through its exclusive focus on the one true love, ends up separating people two by two from any other substantive human relationship."

This chapter dramatically reveals how the Christian fantasy of romance mostly mirrors our contemporary culture, rather than offering a convincing alternative to it. The "perfect Christian love story" is, at best, an unfortunate simulacrum of the gospel. In the end, it calls us away from finding our life in "familial and churchly networks of mutual care and dependence." It obscures the real risks of thoughtful obedience by assuming that "thinking for yourself and trusting in God are mutually exclusive." It serves up an altogether too-sweet appetizer as if it were the meal itself, when it should call us to a genuinely cross-shaped, gospel-centered vision of marriage. The Petersons conclude with wise and practical advice for the whole church on how to imagine marrying and marriage, so that all of us "can come more faithfully and wholeheartedly to think and act and love in ways that are congruent with God's love for us in Christ."

That kind of loving will require a heart and imagination more strongly shaped by the gospel than by Hollywood. Ironically, according to Jason Byassee, we are instead being urged to "look for God eagerly in popular culture." In "God Does Not Entertain," Byassee invites us into critical reflection on the idea that regardless of how God spoke in the past, "in these last days God is speaking through Hollywood." Byassee's response is a "not so fast." He loves the cinema, and it shows in his exposition and examples of how movies "touch us, move us, sometimes motivate us to be better persons." But that does not make a movie an icon or a sacrament, nor does it "mean that God is the Entertainer present in, with, and under every good movie we see. In the end, movies are primarily about entertainment; a movie is still just a movie."

Byassee builds his case carefully. First, he helps us see the difference between the grace God freely offers in Holy Communion and the expense of a movie. If movies are the new sacraments, then we've put a price on grace and fenced out the poor. Next, he helps us to see that the differences between Christian icons and popular movies are far deeper than any surface similarities. That leads to a more extended engagement with two advocates of a sacramental view of cinema. Byassee grants their point that a very interesting conversation about God is occurring in contemporary cinema. But in the end a movie is "not a sacrament. You can't eat it. You oughtn't reverence it. It doesn't make all its partakers one body, nor turn them into Christ's body for the restoration of creation." Though movies are amazing, Byassee closes with an invitation to go to church rather than to meet him at the cineplex. Why? Because "God's church, where God meets us in judgment and grace: that's really where the action is."

If church is where the action is, it is only because there we encounter the Triune God whose very life is ceaselessly enacted as giving and receiving. In the final chapter, I seek to make this point in a thought experiment titled "God Does Father, Son, and Holy Spirit." The essay works by way of negation; it begins by a lengthy critique of efforts to identify the Triune God by the title "Creator, Redeemer, and Sustainer." I suggest that this recent formulation miscounts what God does, which is basically the twofold work of creating and redeeming the world. It also mislocates "Father" as naming primarily God's relation to the world, rather than God's relation to the beloved Son Jesus of Nazareth. Finally, it obscures the way God works in a personal, trinitarian fashion. All three points begin to help us see how "God does who God is."

The remainder of the chapter focuses on unpacking the trinitarian shape of divine doing. What God does in the world has a triune shape, sometimes rendered as "from the Father through the Son in the Holy Spirit." Moreover, God's doing has a triune character, because it flows forth from the ceaseless flow of love that unites these three divine persons. This leads to the suggestion that "God might just as well be named by verbs as by nouns." Why? Because these three simply are by virtue of their ceaseless giving to and receiving from one another. God does Father, Son, and Holy Spirit. I conclude with suggestions of how this makes a difference for the way the church baptizes, worships, is hospitable to difference, and discerns what God does in the world.

This book does not try to expose every caricature of God that runs rampant in the world. There are other distortions of what God does that are every bit as trivial or terrifying as the ones we address here. We do hope that what we offer will provoke vigorous conversation—both about these particular distortions and, more generally, about the church's propensity toward mistaking or misstating what God is doing in the world. In short, we hope that this book can provide training and stimulus for a proper and robust practice of culturally critical theology. We will be pleased if many of our readers also begin to say with us, "God does not . . . !"

God Does Not Wear a White Coat— But God Does Heal

Joel James Shuman

God in a White Coat?

There is a joke common in American hospital culture that has as its setting the hospital cafeteria, where a group of hospital employees are waiting in line to get lunch. Suddenly, an impressive-looking older man with a flowing white beard, wearing a stethoscope and white lab coat, barges in and makes his way to the front of the line, seemingly oblivious to those waiting their turn. One nurse, new to this particular hospital, says to no one in particular, "Who does that guy think he is?" "Oh," says the veteran lab technician behind her in line, shaking his head in resignation, "That's just God. He thinks he's a doctor."

Notwithstanding its questionable assumptions about the appearance and gender of the divinity, this joke seldom fails to elicit a chuckle wherever it is told. Almost everyone, it seems, gets this one, for almost everyone has had an encounter with the medical industry that suggests that wrapped up in the joke's good-natured barb is a kernel of truth. Medical caregivers, physicians in particular, often do attain the status of demigods in the contemporary imagination. Yet this is not primarily the doing of doctors, which is to say that it is not for the most part because physicians have an excessively inflated view of their own importance. Rather, it is because the rest of us have come to believe physicians and their craft are ultimately important, or very nearly so. As a friend says in comparing seminary and medical school educations, "Today no one believes that an incompetent or poorly educated minister could cost them their salvation, but pretty much everyone knows that an incompetent or poorly educated physician could kill them."

The point here is not to disparage medicine or make light of the real good it does, but to call critical attention to the way most of us have come to think about medicine, particularly as it relates to whatever "religious" faith we might profess. In a culture such as our own, when people have such difficulty agreeing about who God is or what God does, God is readily fitted into whatever personae and roles those who still believe in him happen to think most important.[1] And in a time when we are obsessed with physical health and longevity, when medicine is more capable than ever of affording these things to us, and when studies affirming the health benefits of religious behavior seem to appear every day, it is certainly easy to reduce God to the role of doctor. Our tendency is to make God little more than a member of the health care team, one who exists primarily to help us live as long and as free from suffering and disability as we possibly can. This is why it is important for Christians to understand that this is not the God they worship. For even though God can, does, and ultimately will heal us all, God does not wear a white coat.

How God Joined Our Health Care Team

The difference between God's being a doctor and God's being a healer is all but invisible to most of us. We are conditioned to think of healing as first of all a highly individualized, exclusively physiological event, and of medicine (of which doctors are the most visible representatives) as healing's principal, and in most cases its final, source. We imagine medicine, moreover, as not simply highly capable, but predictably so: when we are sick, we go to the clinic or the hospital; we give our insurance information to the receptionist; the nurse takes our history and checks our vital signs; the physician examines us, often by way of some form of sophisticated diagnostic technology; a course of therapy is recommended; we visit the pharmacy (or the surgical suite or the rehab center); and soon we are well again. In extreme cases, where our illness is more serious than can readily be managed locally, the physician refers us to a major medical center, where the doctors are even smarter and better trained, and the technology still more sophisticated. Whatever the case, we expect medicine to make us well, such that the only news that comes as a surprise is the news that nothing more can be done for us.

In such a setting, there is room for "god" only so long as he occupies one or another (or often both) of two roles. First, and probably more typically, "god" is the name given to that which is otherwise intangible, to the remainder that cannot be explained, controlled, or depended upon. God is the one upon whom patients and physicians alike call—to give insight and wisdom to the diagnostician, to steady the surgeon's hand, to make effective the prescribed medications, to calm the heart and quell the fears of the patient, and finally, to intervene when everything else has been tried and has failed. In this vein, God tends to be seen as a kind of uber-specialist, a consultant who may or may not have room on his or her schedule for yet another anxious or desperate patient, a medical version of what theologians and literary critics alike call the *deus ex machina*, or "god of the gaps." If things go well, and we or the people for whom we have been praying get better, we give thanks not just to our doctors but to God, who, after all, is the one who made it (i.e., medicine) all possible. The fact that this is formally true does not make it any less a trivialization of who God is or what God does.

A second, related role given to "god" in the contemporary medical setting is as an allied member of the patient care team. An impressive body of research, much of it done at prominent university medical centers, suggests that patients who engage regularly in behaviors identified as "religious" are healthier than those who do not. Religious patients are sick less often and for shorter periods of time and cope better with illness and its treatment. When such research is interpreted according to the logic of the modern medical industry, which is based increasingly on the predictable reproduction of outcomes, the conclusions are fairly straightforward. If people who regularly participate in religious activities are healthier than those who do not, then those persons who wish to become healthier should participate in religious activities. Religion becomes one treatment modality among others, and "god" is reduced to being an invisible but nonetheless predictably dependable administrator of a newly expanded therapeutic regime.

Recent years have witnessed the publication of a host of popular books and articles advocating just this position, recommending to readers that activities like prayer, meditation, scripture reading, and attendance at religious services are all ways of improving their health. It is worth noting that in most of these works, the emphasis is on particular acts of religious devotion and the intensity of that devotion, rather than the one toward whom the devotion is extended. Readers are encouraged to believe and to practice belief, based on the general assumption that belief itself fosters positive effects on the health of the believer. Says one prominent physician advocate of such practices:

> Apparently, just *having* a strong belief is enough to cause things to happen to our physiology, but this is a very ticklish point. It

does seem that just the state of belief, which can emanate from a variety of personal, philosophical, or religious orientations, is itself a powerful force. Does it matter what you believe in? Belief in *something* is crucial. The very force and effectiveness of your personal belief stem from your basic assumptions that your belief matters. If you want to experience the physiological benefits of the Faith Factor and you have nothing to believe in, it may be helpful to believe generally in the power of life or perhaps even just in the power of belief itself.[2]

God Does Heal

Much could be said about why claims like this have come to carry so much weight among contemporary Christians, not least of which is that they bear a more than passing resemblance to some of what Christians have traditionally said about health and healing. Put simply, God does heal. Christianity, like the Judaism from which it comes, has from the beginning been deeply concerned with health and healing, as signs both of God's love for God's creation and of God's salvific triumph over creation's sin-induced brokenness. The biblical accounts of the reign of God at the consummation of history invariably include allusions to the complete absence of sickness, suffering, and death (Isa. 65:19–20, 66:14; Rom. 8:19–21; Rev. 21:3–6), and Paul refers to the bodies of the resurrected at the end of history as "imperishable" and "immortal" (1 Cor. 15:52–54). According to Luke's Gospel, Jesus's public life as the embodiment of the kingdom of God began with a proclamation of good news to the poor, release to the captives, and recovery of sight to the blind (Luke 4:18–19). His many healings and exorcisms (e.g., Matt. 4:23–25, 8:14–17, 9:2–38 and parallels) are depicted by the Gospel authors as integral signs that in Jesus, God's kingdom had indeed entered into and overcome the brokenness of human history.

The New Testament witness concerning healing is not restricted to the narrative accounts of Jesus's life in the Gospels. Throughout the New Testament health and healing are important concerns for members of the Christian community. Jesus both commissioned his followers to continue his ministry of healing (Matt. 10:1 and parallels) and taught that their care for the sick they encountered would be a lasting sign of their faithfulness to him and the kingdom he proclaimed (Matt. 25:31–46). The Book of Acts, which chronicles the first twenty or so years of the church's existence, is replete with stories of healing as a sign of the presence of God's reign (Acts 3:6–10, 9:36–43, 14:8–11, 20:9–12). Paul understood healing to be among the gifts God had given to the church, which he referred to as the "body of Christ" (1 Cor. 12:9, 12–27). In describing the church as a metaphoric body with Christ as its head, Paul emphasizes the interdependence of the members based on their differences. He regards the mutual sharing of suffering among them as intrinsic to their faithfully representing Jesus's ongoing presence to the world.

The general thrust of biblical references to health and healing, then, is ecological; these texts depict healing as having, in significant measure, to do with restoring and sustaining the sick person's membership among a particular people who understand themselves called together by God into a community where mutual care is one of the signs of God's reign. This means that biblical healing is also fundamentally evangelical, in the sense that it is an expression of the conviction that the particular ways in which the people of God live together and care for one another is intrinsic to their proclamation of the Good News (that is, the gospel) that God has entered into human history and is even now at work healing its brokenness—sometimes miraculously, sometimes in more quotidian ways.

Perhaps, then, the center of gravity for what the Bible has to say about healing may be found in James 5:13–16, which is as remarkable for its association of healing with the ongoing life of the Christian community as for its promise that the sick will be made well:

Are any among you suffering? They should pray. Are any cheerful? They should sing songs of praise. Are any among you sick? They should call for the elders of the church and have them pray over them, anointing them with oil in the name of the Lord. The prayer of faith will save the sick, and the Lord will raise them up; and anyone who has committed sins will be forgiven. Therefore confess your sins to one another, and pray for one another, so that you may be healed. The prayer of the righteous is powerful and effective.

One of the truly significant things about this text is its apparent assumption that at any given time the community will include members who suffer and members who do not, members who are sick and those who are not, and members struggling with the effects of sin and those who are not. Moreover, this dynamic among the membership is presumably contingent and constantly shifting; what remains constant is the recognized commitment of the membership to be present to and for one another: praying, singing, rejoicing, confessing, anointing, and caring. This week one person may be sick and call upon the elders for ministration in the form of prayer and anointing; next week that same person may be among those praying and anointing another member who has fallen sick. The community will always consist of some who are sicker and more dependent and some who are healthier and more depended upon, and while this is never ideal and often unpleasant, it is at least provisionally all right, for among the gifts God has given the members of the church is the gift of each other. Illness is a burden no one needs to bear alone.

It is precisely this subsumption of the healing of sickness within the broader ecological and evangelical character of the Christian community that distinguishes the healing ministry of that community in the centuries following the completion of the biblical texts. Early monasteries and houses of hospitality typically served as places where the sick could come for care, and the sixth-century *Rule of Saint Benedict* devotes an entire chapter to how properly to care for the sick—and to how the sick should properly allow themselves to be cared for. These monastic commitments to caring for the sick served as models for the establishment of the first modern hospitals, many of which were affiliated with Christian communities.[3]

We have here two significant distinctions between the way the relationship of healing to religious faith has historically been understood by Christians and the way that relationship tends to be construed among people of faith in contemporary North American culture. The first of these is that healing viewed through the lens of Christian orthodoxy has to do with more than any one person's mental or physiological state, for the notion "health" involves at its most basic level a set of assumptions about the relationship of a person to his or her community and its place on earth. Thus, as Wendell Berry explains, "the community—in the fullest sense: a place and all its creatures—is the smallest unit of health and . . . to speak of the health of an isolated individual is a contradiction in terms."[4] This leads straightforwardly to a second distinction, which is that in Christian tradition, the health or healing of a given person is generally understood as a limited good in the service of something greater: the gospel claim that, contrary appearances notwithstanding, every momentary triumph of wholeness over disintegration is but one sign that God is at work establishing a reign of wholeness that is not yet fully present to the creation. More simply, the healing we do experience in this life, important as it is, is only a foreshadowing of the absolute healing that will take place at the consummation of God's redemptive work.

God's Wild Faithfulness

Attention to such distinctions ultimately demands that we focus directly on a much more significant matter, namely the identity of the God who heals. Much of the contemporary literature dealing with the relationship of belief to health conforms to the same peculiarly modern logic that facilitates the emergence of modern medicine, which is to say that its focus is on the discovery or development of a technique that will produce predictable, controllable, reproducible results. But the God revealed in the stories of the Bible is anything but a predictable, controllable means of getting what we want. The God we meet in the Bible is a wild God who invites us to become part of a great adventure, namely, the drama leading ultimately to the promised redemption of all creation. In the shorter term, this God promises us only his steadfast faithfulness.

Perhaps the best way of developing some sense of what it means for God to be simultaneously wild and faithful is by attending carefully to the stories of God's self-revelation in scripture, beginning with one of the Bible's best-known stories, that of Moses and the burning bush (Exod. 3:1–22). The broad outline of the story is deeply familiar: The Hebrew Moses, who was raised in the household of the Egyptian Pharaoh, has been exiled to Midian, where he works tending the flocks of his Midianite father-in-law, Jethro. One day, while making his way through the wilderness of Midian, Moses comes upon a bush, engulfed in flame but not burned by the fire. He approaches the bush out of curiosity, and hears a voice from the bush identifying itself as the God of his Israelite ancestors (Abraham, Isaac, and Jacob), admonishing him to remove his shoes (a gesture of reverence) and listen, for he is about to be given an important task. God informs Moses that God has heard the voice of the Israelite people, who have cried out after 400 years of slavery in Egypt, and that he intends to send Moses back to Egypt to demand that Pharaoh release the Israelites from bondage so that they might depart into the promised land of Canaan in fulfillment of God's promise to their ancestors.[5]

But Moses is not persuaded that this is a good idea, for aside from his self-perceived lack of leadership qualities, he is persona non grata in Egypt. Yet, probably because this is God speaking

to him, Moses is unwilling to walk away, and so a negotiation
of sorts ensues. This negotiation centers on what seems to us a
fairly insignificant point; Moses wants to know God's name—but
not just in case someone happens to ask. In the cultural context
within which this text was produced, this question is far from
inconsequential. The peoples of the ancient Near East, most of
whom worshipped the various tribal gods of their ancestors, believed that knowing and using the names of those gods lent to
the user a share of the gods' power. Thus, to know a god's name
was to have a measure of protection from his or her frequent and
sometimes violent capriciousness and to possess the capacity to
wield that capriciousness against one's enemies, who ostensibly
would be the enemies of one's god, as well.[6] Moses, then, has good
reasons for wanting to know the name of the deity who confronts
him in the bush. Not only is the specter of a strange god speaking through a bush that burns but is not consumed sufficiently
terrifying to move one to grasp at whatever trace of control over
that god might be at hand, but the prospect of being sent by that
god on a dangerous mission against a formidable enemy is likely
to inspire the accumulation of an arsenal sufficient to complete
the job.[7]

The conversation that ensues is laden with irony. Moses queries,
"If I come to the Israelites and say to them, 'The God of your ancestors has sent me to you,' and they ask me, 'What is his name?'
what shall I say to them?" God's initial response is elegantly
simple: "I AM WHO I AM." The Hebrew (transliterated *Yahweh*) here
is sufficiently multivalent to lead the reader to wonder whether
God might be engaging Moses in a bit of verbal sparring. For
God's admonition to Moses to tell the Israelites, "I AM has sent
me to you. . . . This is my name forever, and this is my title for all
generations" (Exod. 3:13–15 NRSV), could be read simultaneously
as a refusal by God to play Moses's game and as an assurance that
the identity of the particular God speaking from the bush renders the question irrelevant. Unlike the gods of the surrounding

tribes, this is an altogether different kind of deity, one who can in no way or for any cause be used, but who is also without caprice and therefore absolutely trustworthy. God's faithful presence with (and for) Israel is assured, not because Moses possesses the power that goes along with knowing God's name, but because God, whose character is steadfastly and unconditionally to love his creation, has freely promised it. Israel can therefore be certain that regardless of whatever difficulties face them in their efforts to depart Egypt, I AM will remain their God and ultimately will secure their redemption. God will henceforth be known to Israel first of all by this signal act of liberation; that is, as the God who against all odds delivered them out of Egypt and (re)established them as God's holy people.

One of the earliest deliberations taking place among Christians concerned their relationship to the God who brought Israel out of Egypt. Christians do well to remember the outcome of that debate, which is that the God who reveals Godself to Israel in the Exodus is not other than the God who is present to the creation in Jesus of Nazareth. The God we encounter in Christ is therefore neither less wild nor less faithful than the God Moses encounters in the burning bush, as an episode from the life of Jesus serves to illustrate (Matt. 26:36–56). The setting is the garden at Gethsemane, where Jesus has taken his disciples to pray after their celebration of the Passover meal. Jesus has foreseen and spoken openly of his impending fate—arrest, public humiliation, and execution by crucifixion—and is understandably distressed. This condition is aggravated by the disciples' inability to stay awake while their teacher prays. Just after Jesus finds them sleeping and reproaches them for the third time, a large, heavily armed contingent enters the garden. It is led by the temple establishment, with whom Jesus has had several strident public disagreements over the course of the past week. The mob, or at least its leadership, is intent upon arresting Jesus and subjecting him to an ersatz trial that will end, if they have their way, with his death.

In the midst of the ensuing chaos, one of the disciples, sensing the threat to his teacher and perhaps also to himself, unsheathes his sword and strikes out, cutting off the ear of one of those who have come to seize Jesus.

It is in Jesus's response to this outwardly justifiable act of violence that we are given a sense of God's wild faithfulness not unlike the one we see in the story of Moses and the burning bush.[8] After rebuking the disciple and demanding that he sheathe his sword, Jesus rhetorically asks him to consider a point that is from the perspective of later Christian orthodoxy comparatively obvious, but understandably forgotten in the heat of crisis and on that side of the events of the next few days. "Do you think," he says, "that I cannot appeal to my Father, and he will at once send me more than twelve legions of angels? But how then would the scriptures be fulfilled, which say it must happen in this way?" (Matt. 26:53–54 NRSV). The rest of the story is well known, at least to the marginally biblical literate: Jesus is arrested and his disciples abandon him; he is subjected to the mockery of a "trial" for blasphemy; he is turned over to the Romans, who beat and crucify him for insurrection. On the third day after his burial, his tomb is found empty and he is seen by his followers, risen from death and signaling the onset of a new era of history.

God's Unlikely Healing Rule of History

Like Moses's conversation with God, Jesus's question to his disciples points beyond its immediate situation and asks us to consider other matters, among which is the question of who or what ultimately controls the course and outcome of human history. In both cases, this point is the same. The God of Israel ultimately controls the course of human history, and this toward an outcome that is for the redemption of the entire creation and the restoration of its original wholeness. This does not make the way humans live within history theologically irrelevant, but

radically important, because it means that the people of God—
those called by God to live differently as a testimony to God's
work in the world—are freed from the need to act according to
purely self-interested utilitarian calculations.[9] With respect to
this we may begin and end with the witness of Jesus, who freely
bore the burden of arrest, humiliation, and execution because he
trusted in God's sovereignty over history.[10]

Attending to Jesus as the paradigm for faithfulness directs our
attention to perhaps the most significant characteristic of God's
control of history, which is that it is being accomplished in spite
of all appearances to the contrary. For if we believe, as Christians
throughout history have done, that we have no clearer or more
complete revelation of the identity of the God who rules history
than in Jesus, then we are forced to confront the implication that
God rules history in the unlikeliest of ways. It is not just that
Jesus is born into humble circumstances to an unwed mother,
nor even that he remains poor, lives among the disenfranchised
and despised, openly opposes the political and religious establish-
ments of his day, and rejects violence as a means to bring about
the reign of God he proclaims. It is that he accepts freely the
fate toward which these choices take him, namely, to be arrested
and convicted as an enemy of the empire and to endure death
by crucifixion, a penalty so gruesome that Roman law severely
restricted the class of those who were permitted to suffer it.

On the surface, the crucifixion of Jesus represents a serious
setback to the progress of a social, political, and religious movement that had barely gotten off the ground. Yet this is hardly
the way the authors of the New Testament understand it. Paul,
who concedes in his first letter to the church in Corinth that the
cross of Jesus is superficially both foolish and scandalous, insists
elsewhere that God's power is characteristically made present to
the world in and through human weakness.[11] He makes these
claims not because he believes suffering is in any way good or
because he reckons God takes any pleasure in human suffering,

but because he is convinced that the cross and resurrection of Christ display something fundamental about God's intention for a broken and frequently chaotic world. In his letter to the Colossian church, Paul explains that Jesus is the bodily presence of the God of Israel to the world, the creator of all that exists, and thus properly in authority over all worldly institutions, governments, and powers—one of which, I have argued elsewhere, is medicine (Col. 1:15–20, 2:8–10).[12] Yet, he explains, it is in the cross, and not in spite of it, that this is made manifest to the world. For in the cross, Paul explains, Jesus "disarmed the rulers and authorities and made a public example of them, triumphing over them in it [the cross]" (Col. 2:15). The cross therefore indicates that God's work in and rule over the world is in some measure ironic: through the very act which rulers over the fallen order of the old creation believed they were destroying Jesus and rejecting his new order, God's triumph is made most clear. It is here that Jesus reveals this fallen order fundamentally impotent with respect to its pretension to govern history in anything approaching an ultimate sense. God raises Jesus from death, not to rescue a failed messianic project, but as a fundamental affirmation that Jesus's proclamation and embodiment of the kingdom of God shows us the way the world is supposed to work.[13]

This means that we need to restrain our predilection for drawing conclusions about what God is doing with respect to our personal well-being based on the way things are going at any given moment. We cannot assume that illness is a sign of God's judgment of a particular sick person any more than we can assume that the absence of illness is a particular sign of a person's skill at eliciting God's favor. God is the healer, not simply of this or that person, but of creation in its entirety and of the history through which creation exists. God's healing of the creation is ultimately eschatological, meaning it is assured because of Jesus's death and resurrection and will be fully realized only at the consummation of history when all of creation is conformed to God.

In the meantime, because we are members of a not-yet-perfected creation, our lives will be characterized at least in part by a brokenness that will include some measure of illness and suffering and, eventually, death. Whatever healing we are granted in this life, whether it comes through medicine or miracle, is at once a gift proffered by a gracious God and a sign of God's coming reign. In the interim, suffering is made bearable and healing rendered subservient to faithfulness. This is not because it is good that we suffer, but because our suffering is among those things that are even now being redeemed by the grace of a God from whose love we cannot be separated (Rom. 8:18–39).

God's Healing Church

This is not a theological abstraction but an important practical matter with respect to the way we are called to live our lives as Christian disciples. The insistence that all genuine healing is ultimately an eschatological sign that creation is being restored to its original integrity under God invites us to reconsider what it means to be healthy and to participate in God's healing work. That our word *health* shares a common linguistic ancestry with the words *heal*, *whole*, and *holy* suggests that health is not simply absence of disease but is also integrity of relationship, a particular way of living with other people, with the rest of the creation, and with God.[14] Ultimately, the restoration of these relationships is made possible by God's presence to the world, especially in the community called church. If the biblical witness is taken as representative, the means by which God typically has worked to effect the healing of creation—its salvation, if you will—is through the common life of God's called and gathered people.[15] God's healing work in the world is established primarily (but never exclusively) in and through the social ecology of God's people. In and through the very life together that proclaims God's love to the world, the people of God are given one another as friends pledged to share all manner of burdens, including and perhaps especially illness.

A comprehensive account of this sort of sharing is well beyond the scope of this essay. Yet we can identify at least three particular ways in which the ecology of the body of Christ can represent God's healing presence. First of all, the body of Christ is a community of discernment about the proper uses of medicine. The fact that in baptism Christians are claimed by God and united to God and to one another suggests that decisions about the proper uses of arts like medicine are never purely matters of individual judgment. Saying that medicine is a great gift is not the same as saying that it exists to be used at will. Medicine, like all arts, can be employed in ways inconsistent with the limits that attend our being creatures. As complex and able as modern medicine has become, it is well nigh impossible in many cases to know for certain whether those limits are being approached or have been reached. By placing us in a community of friends who share basic convictions about human goods, God has given us the wisdom of others, some of whom have learned by difficult experience lessons from which we might be spared. As we begin submitting some of our medical decision making to the community, we may find that God speaks to us through the voices of our sisters and brothers.

A second way the body of Christ represents God's healing presence is through the gift of presence. The least sickness isolates us—from our normal daily routines, from our work and our play, and frequently from our families and friends. In such times we need friends who will take time, even at personal expense, to be with us and help us feel human. And when we are seriously ill, when our futures are uncertain and we are tempted more than a little to wonder whether God has abandoned us, we require the presence of others, even when presence is all they can offer. A member of the body of Christ being present, even in painful silence, to a sick person is a sign as well of God's enduring presence. It says, "God has promised never to leave you, and so neither shall we."

Finally, the healing presence of God is represented by the gift of hospitality, the practical help the church can afford to the sick and their families. The world doesn't hesitate, much less stop for us, when we are sick; kids still need to be cared for, meals prepared, houses cleaned, and bills paid. People need rides to the doctor and the pharmacy and sometimes someone to empty their urinals and wipe their butts. These matters and others like them are all reconfigured by membership in the body of Christ, for the fact of our belonging not simply to God but also to one another changes the questions. The kids, houses, meals, and bills are no longer simply mine or yours; rather, they are now ours.

Let me conclude with a personal story I think nicely illustrates the kinds of presence of which I speak. My wife, Chris, and I are members of what I take to be a fairly typical United Methodist Church that has over the past few years gone through a number of difficult transitions. Like a lot of mainline Protestant churches, the seriousness with which a lot of the people (ourselves included) take their Christian faith is not always obvious; in most respects our lives are not much different from those of our neighbors. We have never quite been altogether happy with the church, and yet we have always regarded it as ours, the community of persons with whom we gather to meet God and experience his grace. Each time we have asked ourselves whether we might be happier elsewhere, the answer has been the same: these are our sisters and brothers, and our happiness with them is quite irrelevant to our membership.

Last year was not an easy one for our family. In September we learned that the two foster children who had been living with us and whom we had hoped to adopt were being sent to live with family members. In November I suffered a blood clot and was disabled for several weeks. In January, we opened our home to two new foster children, both toddlers, one of whom proved to have significant behavioral problems. Through all of this, we were constantly impressed by the prayerful concern the church showed us. Then things got really interesting. In March, Chris began experiencing unusually persistent flu-like symptoms. A visit to our family physician led to a battery of diagnostic tests that revealed she suffered from a significant kidney infection. She would have to be hospitalized immediately—and it was 6:00 p.m. We felt, quite simply, helpless. We called our church.

What I remember best about the next few weeks was the presence in our house of dozens of people, some of whom I had barely met. They cooked our meals. They cared for our children. They visited Chris in the hospital, and when she came home they were with her there as well. Whatever we needed, they provided, and more. They were as important to Chris's recovery as the daily antibiotics she was receiving intravenously—literally, a healing presence to our household's suffering and disability. To say the least, we were humbled by the extraordinary grace they extended to us.

Near the end of the illness, when Chris was finally able once again to attend worship, the opportunity arose during the congregation's time of sharing concerns for us to give thanks to those who had cared for us. Chris stood and quietly and tearfully told the congregation that they had given us a gift greater than they could imagine. And she was right, for not only had they met our most basic needs; and not only had they taught us about what it means to be church; they had been for us, and continue to be, agents of the wild, faithful God who heals.

God Does Not Demand Blood

Beyond Redemptive Violence

Daniel M. Bell Jr.

The bow of God's wrath is bent, and the arrow made ready on the string, and justice bends the arrow at your heart, and strains the bow, and it is nothing but the mere pleasure of God, and that of an angry God, without any promise or obligation at all, that keeps the arrow one moment from being made drunk with your blood . . .

Jonathan Edwards,
"Sinners in the Hands of an Angry God"[1]

[Forgiveness] does not annul punitive justice. While mercy is applied to the soul of sinners, it does not set aside the ethical consequences that require "atoning sacrifice." Justice . . . requires a sacrifice, a loss, a deprivation.

J. Daryl Charles, *Between Pacifism and Jihad*[2]

Christians have never embraced blood sacrifice. We have not offered chickens or slain goats, let alone sacrificed our firstborn children to God. Indeed, the very idea of blood sacrifice is abhorrent to us, evoking an almost involuntary, visceral reaction. It sends chills down our spines and stirs deep within us a strong impulse to act against such a horrific practice. I recall well the first time I visited a site where human blood sacrifice was practiced in ages past. I was with a group of Christians. So strong was our revulsion that some in the group simply refused to approach the site, preferring instead to keep a safe distance at the edge. Others entered the site and climbed the steps to the altar, gazing in cold silence at the depression in its stone surface for the victim's heart. Such was the diabolical weight of this site on our imaginations and hearts that none of us was able to talk about the experience for some time. Such is Christian revulsion to blood sacrifice.

Although Christians have never practiced blood sacrifice, the logic of blood sacrifice often shapes the way Christians think about God and, consequently, how we act in the world. From fire-and-brimstone sermons like Jonathan Edward's famous "Sinners in the Hands of an Angry God," to the popular T-shirt sporting an image of Christ crucified with the caption "His Pain, Our Gain," or the blockbuster movie *The Passion of the Christ,* Christianity is permeated with images of a wrathful, angry God who demands blood and suffering and threatens to inflict terrible violence as the just punishment for sin. Our visceral objection to such an image notwithstanding, Christianity frequently communicates the message that God sanctions bloodshed and requires suffering to set things right, to redeem us.

Furthermore, as Christians seek to witness faithfully to God in the world, they reinforce the logic of blood sacrifice whenever they appeal to the divine example so construed to justify or defend social and political practices that draw blood or endorse suffering. God sets the precedent for the necessity of blood and the appropriateness of redemptive violence and suffering in setting things right. Thus, whether it is to defend capital punishment and war, as the evangelical scholar J. Daryl Charles does, or to encourage the abused and downtrodden to patiently endure their affliction, as Martin Luther famously exhorted the impoverished peasants of his day, as church leaders instructed the civil rights activists in the 1960s, and as too many pastors continue to tell too many battered spouses, God is lifted up as the ultimate sanction and source of redemptive violence.

All of this is wrong. This essay argues that God does not demand or require blood to redeem us. God neither inflicts violence nor desires suffering in order to set the divine–human relation right. In spite of its pervasiveness in Christian imagery, the cost of communion, of reconciliation and redemption, is not blood and suffering. Consequently, the justification that is frequently invoked as grounds for Christian support of bloodshed and suffering—namely, "God demands blood and suffering, therefore so should we"—collapses.

Of course, on the surface the claim that God does not require blood and suffering appears patently absurd. After all, is not the cross of Christ the centerpiece or fulcrum of the Christian faith? Consider the prominence of the cross of Christ in the Christian faith—its ubiquitous presence in sanctuaries, in Christian artwork, music and literature, as a ritual gesture made by disciples, as the sign under which Christians are buried, and so forth. Nothing else comes close to capturing the heart of the faith as does the cross of Christ. The cornerstone of the faith is as Paul suggests, "Christ, and him crucified" (1 Cor. 2:2 NRSV). Christ's work of redemption, Christ's atonement, happened on the cross. And the cross was one bloody, violent act.

Therefore, if the argument of this essay is to be persuasive, it must prove its truthfulness in the face of the cross. The claim that God does not demand blood, if it is to hold, must pass through (and not, as some Christian thinkers attempt, over or around) the cross, that most violent and bloody act. By reflecting on the nature and meaning of the cross of Christ and Christ's offering or sacrifice for us, I hope to shed light on what God does indeed desire and how we therefore should live.

The Logic of Blood Sacrifice: Violence Redeems

Before turning to the cross of Christ, however, it is worth lingering for a moment over the logic of blood sacrifice. Here I will briefly unpack what is meant by "blood sacrifice" and consider some of the ways the logic appears in North American society. Of course, I do not mean to suggest that we look for hidden temples of human sacrifice like the one depicted in *Indiana Jones and the Temple of Doom*. Rather, we are looking for a pattern of behavior or a logic of action that posits blood and suffering as a means of setting things right. The logic of blood sacrifice is about the use of violence and suffering as a means to attain an end. In other words, not every sanction for bloodshed or suffering is a matter of what I am calling blood sacrifice. Violence that is, for example, gratuitous (pointless, having no end) is not. Neither is violence for just *any* end or purpose. Thus, bloodshed and suffering that are solely sadistic (intended simply to degrade and humiliate) or purely vindictive do not qualify.

What I mean by the logic of blood sacrifice is captured in the notion of *redemptive violence*. As it was practiced in at least some ancient cultures, blood sacrifice was about violence and suffering that was a means to restoring, protecting, and preserving the order of things. Blood sacrifice was redemptive. When things got out of order due to human transgression, blood sacrifice was offered for the sake of appeasing the gods and restoring that order. In this way, blood sacrifice was part and parcel of protecting, preserving, and restoring life. Violence was redemptive.

Even as we are horrified by the ancient practice of blood sacrifice, all around us we see and hear the message of blood sacrifice reinforced: violence redeems and protects. We are inundated with the message that violence saves, violence secures, violence redeems. Only violence can save us from violence. Good violence is the only thing that protects and preserves us from bad violence.

Blood Sacrifice Today

Thus, since the horrific evil of September 11, 2001, we have been inundated with the message that the only way to protect and preserve our life and lifestyle from terrorism is by unleashing the violence of war on terror. Reason, goodwill, and diplomacy will not save us, we are told. Freedom and democracy can be preserved from the violence of terrorism only by an overwhelming and relentless counterviolence that one pundit called "focused brutality." Furthermore, those who doubt either the morality or the effectiveness of this redemptive violence are dismissed and denounced as not serious, or as liars and hypocrites, or even as evil and terrorists themselves. And if this counterviolence means curtailing democracy and other freedoms, if it means locking up folks indefinitely, rounding up their family members as well, and torturing suspects, so be it. After all, what is at stake is our very survival; this is what is required to save us.

On the domestic front, faith in redemptive violence is displayed in a variety of ways as well. In the wake of the recent shooting on a college campus, in the state where I live signs appeared on the side of the road urging us "Vote 'Yes' to Guns in Schools," and several bills to that end were introduced in the state legislature, a move that was echoed on national airwaves where easier recourse to violence was trumpeted as the solution to such horrible acts. These efforts, of course, are in line with social trends in recent years that stress "law and order," that revolve around the notion that only violence can save us from violence. Hence, the push for more police and prisons, with the police being militarized and the prison conditions made more draconian. Accompanying these efforts are moves toward longer prison sentences, the expansion of the death penalty, and removing barriers to the military's involvement in domestic law enforcement.

Culturally, the message that violence saves is perhaps nowhere more evident than in movie theaters and on the television screen. The plot of countless shows and movies can be summed up as "People who use bad violence are pursued by people who use good violence, and, in the end, good violence saves the day." The paradigmatic example of this is the classic Western film *High Noon*, which reaches its climax as the pacifist character played by Grace Kelly comes to her senses and embraces violence to save her husband and the town. But every generation has its media icon of redemptive violence, from Dirty Harry and Rambo to the *Lethal Weapon* and *Die Hard* franchises to Jack Bauer of the current hit show *24*. Although the names and faces change, the message is constant: Only through violence is law and order maintained; only violence saves us from the worst violence.

Besides these rather straightforward examples, we receive, enact, and reinforce the conviction that violence is redemptive in a host of more subtle and indirect ways. Consider, for example, how quickly we resort to the language of violence, and particularly war, to address a host of problems and issues. Thus, we lament the "culture wars" or praise the "war on drugs." In the not-too-distant past, we waged a "war on poverty." Today we grieve someone losing their "battle" with cancer, or the headlines announce a "war on pain," or a school introduces a "battle of the bulge" to counter (I almost wrote "combat") childhood obesity. Christians who think youth culture is headed in the wrong direction start a movement called "Battle Cry for a Generation." A local church announces a teaching series on interpersonal relations with the title, "Love Means War." A school administrator does not agree with the position a teachers' union takes and so denounces its members as "terrorists." A pastor in training remarks that when his wife gets out of line, "Well, I have a two-by-four for that." Children's bibles are covered in camouflage with "God's Army"

stitched on the cover. Infants and toddlers are decked out in
military fatigues. The most popular video games revolve around
apocalyptic levels of violence. (And in an interesting twist, writes
Lt. Col. David Grossman, the military is now copying civilian
culture in this regard and using video games in its training.)[3] A
few years ago retailers were selling martial Easter baskets—pastel
baskets stuffed with gun-toting soldiers, tanks, knives and gre-
nades, accompanied by a card reading "Happy Easter." Although I
suspect the retailers did not think about this, those martial baskets
were profoundly appropriate symbols of our culture's conviction
that violence, and not the risen Christ, redeems.

Redemptive Suffering

Thus far, we have considered how violence is thought to be
redemptive in terms of its being *inflicted upon* others. This is to
say, by far the most popular notion of redemptive violence is
framed in terms of how it is sometimes necessary to inflict violence on others to secure and protect a good. It is necessary to kill
someone else to save myself and those I love. There is, however,
another side to our belief in the redemptive power of violence
that is not as prominent but is nevertheless part of our public
discourse and imagination. This side holds that sometimes it is
redemptive to *suffer* violence. It is necessary that I suffer or even
die to save myself or others. While much of our popular discourse
expresses a strong aversion to suffering, and so defends the resort
to inflicting violence on others to save ourselves from suffering,
there is nevertheless a clear undercurrent that affirms suffering
violence to make things right.

Often, this side of the belief in the redemptive power of violence
comes to the fore when we are confronted with what is commonly
called the problem of evil. Why do the innocent suffer? Why do
bad things happen to good people? Why did God allow this illness or accident or tragedy or crime to happen? Faced with the

problem of suffering, of violence that is suffered, it is frequently said—both by victims and by those who would console them—that suffering violence can be redemptive. Suffering violence becomes redemptive insofar as it is said to be cleansing, purgative, or purifying. In its most blunt form, suffering violence is redemptive as suffering becomes a means of paying for or being purged of one's sin. One suffers because one has sinned, and by undergoing the violence of suffering or suffering violence, one compensates or pays the price for one's sin, thereby restoring the moral order and assuring one's redemption.

A second way in which suffering violence is said to be redemptive concerns what we might call the educative or pedagogical function of suffering. If the first version of redemptive suffering holds that the victim deserves to suffer and by suffering is redeemed, this version does not blame the victim or suggest that the victim deserves to suffer violence. Instead, suffering violence is said to be redemptive insofar as through the experience one can learn and grow. Many of us have been told that suffering hardship "builds character." As a young person once told me, by suffering the bad, we can better appreciate the good, just as we can know the beauty of sunshine only if we have experienced the bleakness of the thunderstorm. In more sophisticated forms, this argument suggests that humans are created by God with a vast reservoir of physical, moral, and intellectual potential that is stimulated and developed only by struggling against and finally overcoming tragedy and evil.

A third form of this vision of redemptive suffering revolves around the ways in which suffering is a prerequisite for some reward or greater good. Here, suffering violence is redemptive in the sense that it is compensated. This version neither blames the victim nor insists that we learn something from suffering. Instead, it simply holds that there is a compensation or reward attached to suffering violence. If we suffer, then we will receive a reward. Suffering becomes the price, if you will, of the sought-after reward. This is the message of redemptive violence that is sometimes presented to the poor and oppressed. An impoverished woman once shared with me that her church had told her that her suffering on this earth was God's will, that she should not act or expect things to change, and that she would be rewarded in heaven. Likewise, it is not uncommon for battered spouses to report that when they told their pastor about the abuse they were suffering, the pastor encouraged them to go home and be a better spouse. The message here is that suffering is either cleansing (the spouse deserves it because she was not being a good wife) or compensatory in that by being a better spouse she may contribute to the redemption of her wayward husband. One might interpret the white clergy's exhortation to Martin Luther King Jr., while he was in the Birmingham jail, along the same lines. King and his coworkers were told not to press for change so hard, to wait, to continue to suffer the violence of white supremacy, and that by doing so they would be compensated by the eventual end of the reign of white supremacy.

Another form of this compensatory version of redemptive suffering is very popular, if a bit more abstract. I am referring to what is popularly called the "free will defense" of suffering. Suffering is redemptive insofar as it is necessarily linked to that great good which is free will. Innocent suffering is rewarded or redeemed by the surpassing goodness of the gift of free will. Granted, God could have eliminated the possibility of our suffering violence at the hands of others or ourselves, so the argument goes, if God had created us as robots, without free will. Instead, God bestowed upon us in creation the gift of free will, and having free will necessarily entails the risk of suffering violence at the hands of either others or ourselves. Here again, as in the other examples above, suffering violence is redemptive insofar as it is compensated or rewarded by a greater good with which it is necessarily linked.

The logic of blood sacrifice holds that violence saves. Whether it is a matter of inflicting violence on others to protect, preserve, or restore the good and the right or of encouraging others to suffer violence for the sake of some redemptive benefit, the message that violence redeems is pervasive. But is it correct?

"Behold the Lamb Who Was Slain": Violence, Redemption, and the Cross of Christ

Maybe this is exactly as it should be. Maybe there is absolutely nothing wrong with believing in redemptive violence, in believing that violence saves. After all, at the center of the Christian faith stands a profound act of violence—the cross. Granted, we can easily forget this, having turned the cross into a pretty piece of jewelry that can pass for "bling" in pop culture. Perhaps we should take the advice of one pastor I heard and hang an electric chair from the ceiling at the front of our churches. Then we might recall the horrific violence of the cross. Actually, Mel Gibson may have saved the churches the significant expense in remodeling costs with his hit movie *The Passion of the Christ*. There, we are confronted with the cross stripped of its precious metals and gemstones, of its colorful banners and Easter lilies, reminded in no uncertain terms that the cross was a brutally violent act. And was it not the supreme act of redemptive violence? Is it not the case that in spite of our visceral reaction against blood sacrifice, Christ was indeed the ultimate blood sacrifice? Is it not the case that, as an acquaintance remarked upon seeing Gibson's movie, Jesus saves because he suffered more violence than anyone? The cross is a stark reminder that redemption is the result of maximum violence.

Although Gibson's movie was an exceptionally (and some would say, excessively) graphic display of the violence connected with Christ's work of redemption or atonement on the cross, it is not that different from one of the prominent, if not the dominant, accounts of how Jesus saves that is taught and preached in countless churches. I remember being taught it while growing up in the church, although I certainly would not have known it by its technical name, and I have heard it repeated countless times since then. The account is frequently called the "satisfaction" or "substitutionary" theory of atonement, and it is attributed to the medieval theologian Anselm. Its argument goes something like this: In the face of human sin, which is an offense against God's honor, God, as one who must uphold justice, cannot simply forgive sin but must enforce a strict rendering of what is due. Because sinful humanity cannot fulfill its debt, the God-man, Christ, steps forward and fulfills justice, renders what is due, through his substitutionary death on the cross. In this way, redemption is a result of the payment of a debt incurred through sin by means of a compensatory death that satisfies divine justice.

A slightly different theory, called the "governmental," replaces the notion of God's "honor," which strikes many modern people as a rather quaint and antiquated notion, with the concept of the moral order of the universe. Thus, we are told, sin is a rupture of the moral order of the universe, and if God were to merely pardon or overlook that breach, then the moral order—right and wrong—would collapse. There would be no consequences for sin, and subsequently no incentive for people to live a moral life. Social life, indeed civilization itself, would be undermined, as murder and other crimes would go unchecked. Hence, Christ suffers the violence of the cross and dies in order to uphold the integrity of moral order of the universe.

In either case, whether Christ dies in order to satisfy God's offended honor or to maintain the moral order of the universe in the face of human sin, violence is the fulcrum of redemption. In either case it was necessary that violence be inflicted and suffered in order for redemption, restoration, and salvation to be effected. In the face of wrong, these theories tell us that only blood can set things right. In the face of sin and evil, only violence inflicted and suffered can restore the moral law and order. Thus Christ's work on the cross is the paradigmatic example of redemptive violence.

Christ is the great blood sacrifice offered to God as a substitute for us. Christ diverts the arrow of an angry deity's wrath from our hearts by stepping in front of it and letting it plunge into his own. Justice requires a loss, a deprivation, a blood sacrifice. Only the blood of the Lamb saves us from the fiery hell we so richly deserve.

What Is Wrong with Redemptive Violence?

One way to deal with the cross while making the case that God does not demand blood is simply to reject it. Some reject out of hand the cross and any sense in which the cross of Christ was redemptive or central to the story of how God redeems in this world. Some appeal to love and argue that a God of love would not demand blood, and that therefore the traditional focus on sacrifice and the cross of Christ is in error. Some point out how the traditional account of Christ's atoning work is analogous to child abuse—a father brutally tortures and kills his child because of the transgressions of other children—and how it has been used to sanction and legitimate all sorts of terrible practices down through history, not least of which encouraging the downtrodden and abused to passively accept their lot in life.

Yet any effort to make the case that God does not demand blood cannot simply skip over the cross but instead must pass right through it. This is the case not just because efforts to circumvent the cross run against the grain of the tradition and jettison significant portions of scripture, but because discarding the cross and talk of atonement through the blood of the Lamb also undercuts the laudable goals of those who reject blood sacrifice. In other words, we need the cross of Christ in order to reject the logic of blood sacrifice.

Allow me to explain how simply rejecting Christ's work of atonement, his cross, works against efforts to end redemptive violence. Let us consider, first, the temptation of Jesus in Luke 4,

and then Martin Luther King Jr.'s advocacy of redemptive suffering in the struggle to overcome white supremacy. In the fourth
chapter of Luke, Jesus is tempted by the devil. Now, because the
devil is involved, we know that the proper thing for Jesus to do
is to stand fast against the temptations. Unfortunately, however,
our reflection typically stops there as we draw a moral along the
lines of "because Jesus resisted temptation, so can and should
we," or we take this as an object lesson about Jesus: that he is
our buddy because he is like us, subject to temptation. We rarely
go on to probe what was wrong with the devil's challenges. The
devil challenges Jesus to turn a stone into bread in the wilderness, an act reminiscent of Israel's being fed in the wilderness.
And what is wrong with that? After all, we know that Jesus will
indeed provide the bread of life that nourishes the world. Then
the devil offers Jesus all the kingdoms of the world. Again, what
is wrong with that? We know that Christ is the king, that Christ
is indeed Lord of all the principalities and powers of this world.
So what is the problem? And finally the devil challenges Jesus to
put on a display of divine power and favor. And again, what is
wrong with that? After all, Jesus is the Son of God who is rightly
the center of worship and who is not only protected by angels but
resurrected! The problem is that the devil offers Jesus a path to
good things—feeding the world, ruling the world, worship—that
circumvents the cross. This passage suggests that it is the devil
who wants a Jesus without a cross (something captured in Nikos
Kazantzakis's novel *The Last Temptation of Christ*). Why is this?
If Christ's journey to the cross is indeed about upholding blood
sacrifice and violence, then why is the devil trying to get Jesus
to turn away, to take a short cut, if you will? After all, brutality
and violence are the devil's thing. The devil should want Jesus to
die on the cross instead of trying to get him to set it aside. And
what is it about Christ's work that would be fatally flawed, to the
point that he would be worshipping the devil as Luke suggests,
if he were to take the shortcut and skip Golgotha?

Consider too Martin Luther King Jr.'s advocacy of redemptive suffering.[4] At first glance, King's advocacy of suffering could be interpreted as problematic, insofar as it appears to be a perfect example of the logic of blood sacrifice. He seems to encourage suffering, and he declares that it can be redemptive. Is this not a perfect example of blood sacrifice and redemptive violence? But, alas, what would have happened to King and the civil rights movement if they had heeded the calls to set aside the cross? How much tighter might be the bonds of white supremacy today if he and the faithful Christians who joined him in the streets, facing the billy clubs and fire hoses and dogs, had rejected the call to imitate Christ and his sacrifice? Where would so many of the saints be if they had refused to bear their cross in faithful imitation of Jesus?

What these two cases suggest is that simply circumventing the cross may not lead as straightforwardly as some might think to the results desired, namely, the end of bloodshed, suffering, and violence. At least if Luke 4 is anything to go by, we should be suspicious of claims that the desired end can be attained by avoiding the cross. Furthermore, as King realized, simply rejecting suffering may cut the nerve of the kind of faithful engagement needed to overcome suffering and blood sacrifice.

These cases, however, even as they suggest problems with simple rejections of the cross and sacrifice and the atoning work of Christ, finally do not answer what we are to make of the cross if we cannot simply discard it. Here we consider the suggestion that rejecting Christ's work on the cross is unnecessary. A word of caution is in order. By suggesting that Christ's atoning work on the cross should not be dismissed, the point is decidedly not that the concerns expressed by folks who reject Christ's work on the cross and atonement and sacrifice are misguided. To the contrary, at least some of the concerns are on target. One would hope, for example, that those who feel compelled to retain the centrality of Christ's atonement would also feel the force of the criticisms leveled at the cross for the ways in which is has been used/abused to sanction all sorts of horrible acts.

The challenge is to retain the importance of Christ's atonement in a manner that does not sanction abuse and brutality. Why? Not merely out of regard for prevailing social currents and sensitivities of the day, but because, as I will show momentarily, when understood rightly, Christ's work of atonement itself calls for the rejection of blood sacrifice and the logic of redemptive violence. This is to say, because Christ's work on the cross is *not* about satisfying a divine demand for blood, because Jesus's saving work is all about showing us that God does *not* demand blood, it cannot be faithfully used to provide either a cover for human bloodshed or a redemptive mantle for the passive suffering urged upon the downtrodden and abused. Far from reinforcing blood sacrifice and redemptive violence, Christ's work on the cross is nothing less than the divine *refusal* of blood sacrifice, as well as any notion that suffering violence is or can be redemptive.

Rereading the Tradition, Rethinking Christ's Work on the Cross

All of this is to say that the dominant understanding of Christ's work on the cross, what was called the satisfaction or substitutionary view, which makes of Christ's work a blood sacrifice, is wrong. Care is needed here, for I am not suggesting that either Anselm or Paul was wrong. Far from it. What I am suggesting is that the dominant understanding of Christ's work as a blood sacrifice that makes satisfaction to God, either to appease God's wrath or to reinforce the moral order, is a distortion of both Anselm and Paul. The belief that violence redeems, the belief that it is Jesus's violent death that saves us, is a terrible corruption of the Christian vision of both God and redemption. That God the Father would save us by inflicting violence on the Son is divine child abuse. And God is not an abuser. God does not demand blood, either as punishment or to maintain the moral order.

Shorn of distortions widespread and longstanding in both popular and scholarly circles, Anselm reveals not the bloody horror but the radiant beauty of the relentless love that seeks to redeem us.[5] Read rightly, Anselm's account of how humanity is redeemed by Jesus satisfying God's honor is not about diverting the arrows and appeasing the wrath of a bloodthirsty, angry god. Nor is it about the necessity of punishment, of loss and deprivation to make things right. Rather, it is a love story from beginning to end. It is the story of the depths and lengths to which the love of God goes so that we might share in the love that is the communion of the triune life of God. It is the story of God's relentless, longsuffering love for us (John 3:16).

According to Anselm, God became human not so that there might be a suitable object on which to vent the divine wrath, nor in order to meet the demands of an implacable moral order before which even God must bow, but so that humanity might be restored to the place of honor that God from the beginning intended for humanity, namely, participation in the divine life (2 Pet. 1:4). This is to say, God became human in order that God's original desire in creating humanity—communion—might be brought to fruition. As Anselm says, God created humanity for blessedness, and it just does not make any sense that God's will should be thwarted by human sin. In this regard, the injury that sin causes to God's honor is a matter of the absence of humanity from full communion with its Creator. Thus, rightly understood, God's honor is not a barrier to humanity's reconciliation with God (as though God were an offended aristocrat); rather, it is the origin of God's free act to provide humanity with a path to renewed communion. Whereas according to the logic of blood sacrifice, injured honor requires compensatory or retributive suffering, according to the logic of divine charity God's honor requires the redemption of alienated humanity so that it might share in the communion for which it was created. Accordingly, the atonement and Christ's work on the cross displays the fullness of divine charity, of the lengths to which God will go to renew communion, even in the face of our bloody rebellion. The work of atonement is God in Christ bearing human rejection and extending the offer of grace again, thereby opening a path for humanity to recover blessedness. In this sense, Christ's faithfulness even to the point of death on the cross marks not a divine demand for retribution, but a divine refusal to hold our rebellion against us. God offers us life and we reject it. God continues to offer it, in the form of love incarnate, and we crucify him. Yet even now, God will not lash out against us but instead raises Jesus up and sends him back with the same offer of life. Christ is God bearing offense, even the offense of the cross, without holding it against us, without giving up on us, without exacting compensation or inflicting retribution, instead continuing to extend the offer of communion. Christ's work of atonement, including the cross, is nothing less than God refusing our refusal; Christ is God rejecting our rejection and instead continuing to offer us the gift of life and love. Even after we crucified him.

None of this means that Anselm's vision should not be linked to a notion of satisfaction and substitution. What it does mean is that the nature and meaning of the satisfaction and substitution Christ offers need to be rethought. What satisfies God is not blood. God takes no joy and garners no satisfaction from the death of even the wicked; rather, what satisfies God is fidelity, obedience, and devotion (Ezek. 18:23). So Christ is our substitute, but not in the sense that Christ takes our place in the execution chamber and suffers our punishment for us. Rather, he is our substitute in the sense that he offers to God the fidelity, devotion, and obedience that we should have but did not, and subsequently could not.

Paul holds a similar vision of Christ's work on the cross, although like Anselm he has been and continues to be subject to a terrible misreading. After all, it is commonplace to read the early chapters of his Epistle to the Romans in terms of a blood sacrifice, as if Christ died because an angry god demanded blood as payment and punishment for human transgressions (cf. Rom. 3:25, 5:9). Such a reading of Paul, however, profoundly distorts the good news that he preached and literally staked his life upon. In this regard, consider a passage from another of Paul's letters:

> Let the same mind be in you that was in Christ Jesus,
> who, though he was in the form of God,
> did not regard equality with God
> as something to be exploited,
> but emptied himself. . . .
> And being found in human form,
> he humbled himself
> and became obedient to the point of death—
> even death on a cross.
>
> (Phil. 2:5–8 NRSV)

It is thought that this passage of Paul's comes from a hymn that was part of the worship of the early church, and it is the last part of the verse that is of particular importance for understanding Christ's work on the cross and how God does not demand blood: "he humbled himself and became obedient to the point of death—even death on a cross." Because we live in a world where the logic of blood sacrifice prevails, it is perhaps understandable that when we look at the cross, and even when we read scripture, it is the violence that catches our eye, and we think that violence is what redeems us. But as Paul points out, echoing the worship of the early church, it is not a blood sacrifice that saves us. What saves us? Jesus saves us. More specifically, Jesus's obedience and fidelity—Jesus's faithfulness saves us.

What does God desire? Not blood and suffering and death, but love, worship, obedience, fidelity, friendship. What God wants is what God has always wanted from us—it is why God created us in the first place—friendship/communion. This is the message of Romans.[6] Paul writes to the church in Rome in anticipation of his visiting them, and he writes to address a question that this predominantly Gentile congregation has: Why should we trust God if this God once made a covenant promise to the Jews but now appears to have rejected them in favor of us Gentiles? Is God trustworthy? Paul's answer is that God is just, and by this Paul means that God is faithful to God's promises. He argues (in chapters 1–3) that no one ever deserved the promise, that the promise was always a matter of faith (chapter 4), and that Jesus is the embodiment of God's faithfulness to the divine desire for communion and reconciliation (chapter 5). Jesus was obedient to this divine mission of reconciliation and communion, even when faced by human resistance and rejection in the form of the brutality of the cross.

When Christ and the cross are interpreted in terms of the logic of blood sacrifice, God becomes a problem. Either God's pride or God's merciless moral order becomes an obstacle to human redemption. God's pride and anger stand between us and blessedness. And Jesus is the innocent victim who solves the problem by suffering redemptive violence. Yet as the Christian (and Jewish) story reminds us, God is not rightly cast as the obstacle but is the source and vehicle of human redemption. The one constant in the biblical narrative is God: No matter how stubborn humanity is, no matter how frequently it rebels and turns away, God's love is steadfast. Actually the term is *longsuffering*, and Christ in his life, death, and resurrection, is the final faithful, obedient embodiment of this longsuffering divine love. What God desires is not blood, but life, love, and communion.

"Let the Same Mind Be in You"

Why did God become human? Not because God was angry and wanted to lash out violently and draw blood. No—"for God so loved the world . . ." Jesus is the embodiment of God's forgoing wrath for the sake of communion. Jesus comes to us in love to renew the friendship/communion that we rejected. Jesus comes to us with the offer of friendship with God. It is not the violence of the cross that saves us. Rather, it is the love of God expressed in Jesus that saves us. It is the love that would rather die on the cross than give up on us—either by fleeing from us or by calling down legions of angels to slay us.

Right? We reject God, so God sends Jesus with the offer of life again, and when we reject it again, Jesus could have just abandoned us. Or he could have called down fire from heaven to destroy us. But he did not. He remained faithful to his mission, still reaching out to us till the bloody end: "Father, forgive them . . ." As Paul says, Christ humbled himself, accepting the humiliation of death rather than give up on us. What saves us is the love that is so determined to reach us that it remains faithful and obedient to its mission even in the face of death. It is the love of God in Christ that saves us; not the violence of the cross. There is no good violence in the cross. There is no redemptive violence. Only steadfast, relentless, and longsuffering love redeems.

If the cross was not the violence of God, and if God did not nail Jesus to the cross, then who did? Who nailed Jesus to the cross? Who demands blood? Who demands a heart to sink the knife of retribution into? Who insists that atonement require a loss and deprivation? Who insists that only a blood sacrifice can restore the moral law and order? In many churches there is a Good Friday service, during which the congregation answers this question. As we listen to the passion narrative, there is a moment when we are invited to respond with the naked truth about our sinful selves. Confronted with the love that refuses to give up on us, we join the crowd of humanity, yelling: "Crucify him! Crucify him!" Who demands blood? Who tries to impose and enforce the logic of blood sacrifice? We do. We killed Jesus. Humanity in rebellion.

Yet, as Paul and Anselm show, Christ came precisely to provide a way beyond this order of blood and suffering. Christ puts an end to the logic of blood sacrifice by bearing the offense of sin and refusing to respond in kind. In this way, as the author of Hebrews suggests, Christ is the last sacrifice for sin (Heb. 7:27, 10:10, 12). He is the advent of the end of blood sacrifice.

Thus, as we are joined to Christ and made part of his body, we are not somehow submitting to the logic of blood sacrifice. We are not simply being let off the hook for our sin by deflecting the punishment for that sin onto someone else. We are not satisfying an angry god by throwing that god a piece of innocent red meat. Nor are we offering a bloody sacrifice for the sake of reinforcing how important the moral law and order are.

Rather, as we are *joined* to Christ we become a people who are transformed (sanctified) and so live our lives according to another, merciful logic. As Paul wrote to the churches in his day, "Let the same mind be in you that was in Jesus Christ." Some translations render this as, "Let this mind be in you that you have in Christ." The point is that in Christ we are not just pardoned but are also healed of our sin and transformed. We are made a different kind of people, a new creation, who live by a different logic. So we love our enemies and pray for those who persecute us. We forgive, just as we have been forgiven. We renounce violence as a means of defending or securing or saving ourselves or those we love. After all, to the extent that our savior is Christ, then our defense, security, and salvation depend on Christ and the love that overcomes enemies through the power of the resurrection. In Christ we become a people who live out the same relentless, fearless, hopeful love that was in Christ, re-fusing to give up, even on our enemies, even in the face of the cross. This is to say, in the midst of a very violent world with its logic of blood sacrifice, which has not stopped erecting crosses in the name of redemptive violence, we are called and empowered to live out the ministry of reconciliation (2 Cor. 5:17–20). In a world that demands blood, that insists only violence can save us from violence, we point to a savior who redeems not by taking life, but by giving it.

Now, there is much more that needs to be said but cannot in this brief essay about this ministry of reconciliation and the logic of charity that underwrites it. For example, this way of life is sacrificial, but the sacrifice God desires is not that of a loss and deprivation. Rather, it is the sacrifice of praise and thanksgiving, obedience and faithfulness. Of course, it does not take much imagination to see that this way of life, this sacrifice of praise and faithfulness, may entail enduring suffering, even bearing the cross. That this is the case, however, is not because suffering is in some way good or redemptive. If we suffer in this way of life, it is not because this is what God wants or because it is punishment for our sin. After all, scripture and tradition are clear that we cannot pay for our sin (Ps. 49:7). Rather, insofar as we are told to be prepared to suffer on the way of discipleship, it is because suffering is the cost that *humans* in their sinful rebellion impose on other humans. In other words, suffering is a contingent cost that humans impose. Suffering is the will of fallen humanity, not God.

Moreover, even as we are called to be prepared to suffer, this does not mean either that we seek out suffering or that we must always passively endure suffering. There is a difference between bearing suffering and bearing it in order to bear it away.[7] Furthermore, the merciful logic of this way of life, which refuses the violent logic of blood sacrifice, does not thereby simply reject justice, accountability, or discipline. On the contrary, this way of life is disciplined, accountable, and seeks justice; it may include practices such as incarceration or even just war.[8] But what this justice and discipline look like, shaped as they are by the charity and mercy of God, will be significantly different from the so-called justice and discipline that belong to the law and order of blood sacrifice.[9]

All around, the children of Cain, Lamech's siblings, are locked in a furious civil war, spilling blood and spreading suffering, planting fields of crosses. All the while, they insist that this is what God demands. God demands bloody retribution for sin. God's moral order requires violent satisfaction. God desires loss and deprivation. Blood sacrifice is the only way that our life, our loved ones, our future can be saved, secured, protected, and preserved. So they insist.

In the midst of their frenetic warring and cross making, they do not notice God, battered and broken, hanging on one of those crosses. The very God in whose name they are busy making all these crosses hangs there with all the crucified, not because that is what he demands, but rather because he desires life, even life for the ones who crucify him, and he refuses to let go of this hope, this desire, this love, even if it kills him.

"For I have no pleasure in the death of anyone, says the Lord GOD. Turn, then, and live."[10] God does not require blood. Life is what God desires; life is what God gives us in Christ. Let the same mind, the same desire be in us.

God Does Not Hurry

Kelly Johnson

Gods Who Hurry

Superman would make a terrific god. On hearing of robbery, kidnapping, or plans to obliterate whole cities, he leaps into action, soars through the air, races against time to rescue the innocent victim and make short work of the villain. He does not hurry because he is our hero: he is our hero because he hurries. "Faster than a speeding bullet" is impressive under any circumstances, but exercised in a time of danger, when every moment counts, it takes on a kind of salvific importance. He races against death, and he wins. In fact, in the 1979 *Superman: The Movie*, he rushes to prevent a series of catastrophes, only to find that in spite of all his successes, he had failed to save Lois's life. Rather than accept his limitation, in a burst of grief he races as never before and manages to turn back time. He saves her and rescues himself from the horror of failing to be the hero. Superman does not just stand against a few notable criminals. He takes on our great nemesis—the relentlessly one-way march of time, which turns everything into dust. He hurries and therefore saves.

The enduring appeal of the superhero genre reflects a longing that runs deep: the desire for a god who hurries. This is not the same as a desire for a god who is fast. Hurry is less about simple speed than about overcoming every obstacle to speed; to hurry is to act energetically against whatever might slow one down. We may sprint just for the pleasure of the speed, but when we sprint through an airport we do it as a struggle against obstacles to our need. Our hurry is a kind of enmity toward anything that gets in our way—other passengers included. Hurry pushes through or runs over every obstacle for the sake of getting to the goal faster.

What's the source of this enmity? It is our sense of being endangered, imperiled by lack of time. But this danger and the enmity that comes with it fuel our love of heroes. The greater the danger, the greater the heroism. Indeed, the hero himself or herself must be in danger, superpowers notwithstanding. Every superhero has his or her version of kryptonite and some arch-foe that ensures the hero really faces danger. It is part of the appeal of Superman that he shares not only our grief and rage, but also our fear and, ultimately, our vulnerability. He differs from us only in that he has the strength and the courage to run into the midst of danger and, in the nick of time, to defeat it, just barely. We long for a god who hates and fears as we do, but who, unlike us, can overcome even time itself, though just barely. Our need for and love of such heroes depends on our sense that we live in a world whose deepest reality is a life-threatening lack of time, a world in which we must hurry.

Contrary to claims that heroism is dead, this kind of heroism abounds, on screen and off. Police, firefighters, and emergency room doctors must act against the danger of time slipping away, and we honor them for their energy and nerve. In fact, this image of a god who both is and is not one of us may be much indebted to the examples of real people, like the firefighters who rushed into the World Trade Center as it burned.

This is, we all know, a futile heroism. Mortality means that time does run out. At the "last call" of our lives, we may go willingly or reluctantly, but we will go. The very deadline that gives meaning and incentive to the struggle is always in danger of dissolving meaning and incentive. Heroes run a good race, but death will finally beat them all.

In the face of that deadline, hurrying becomes a kind of token of vigor and creativity. Seize the day! A commentator noted recently that for the bright and brave in Vietnam these days, the stress (or "si-tress") of being overwhelmed with new tasks and not enough time is a badge of honor. "Listening to my countrymen, I cannot help but detect a touch of bragging in the familiar complaints. When a Vietnamese says he is 'si-tress,' he is also saying, 'It's the new world, but I'm successful, thriving and busy, and this is the price I'm willing to pay for it.'"[1] Stress means I have something important to do. Little wonder, then, that for all the complaining we do about being stressed, few of us make significant changes to our pace. Our stress is our chance at stardom, our share in heroism, our way of fighting the good fight. We who are in a hurry have important things to do. It begins to seem that only sick or aged or uninteresting people are not in a hurry, for who else would be content to endure the passage of time without a fight? Sitting still and waiting is tedium, a frustrating loss of opportunity, a waste.

In fact, this heroic war with time appears in much more mundane ways all around us. Families find themselves struggling to "capture the moment" via photo and video, and parents do whatever it takes to keep their kids in cell-phone contact, just in case. What if the kids were sick or the car broke down and they needed help quickly? Bad things can happen quickly, and the work of justice has to take speed as an ally. That's how the marketing works, and it does work. These potential moments of crisis and our fears about them then begin to drive the ordinary moments of life. The fast-food industry, for example, appeared out of the confluence of technical development of military cuisine in World War II and the development of the interstate highway system.[2] A style of cooking and eating developed for crises moved into civilian life and became the norm.

In this way, moral heroism is tangled up in technological invention. New tools make ordinary cops capable of superhero achievements; improvements in communication and travel have made a sort of "wrinkle in time," so that people around the world can make common cause on issues that concern them. Medical technology pushes at the boundaries of human finitude. Life is expanded in length, in comfort, and in possibilities.

But to be precise, technological invention is not the hurry of a hero, driven by compassion or self-sacrificing love or a determination to rage against the dying of the light. The speed of technology is in itself only about getting a job—any job—done with maximum efficiency, smoothly, powerfully, quickly. Without any romantic fanfare, the equipment transmits information, performs complex calculations, analyzes data. It has no goal except more efficiency. That does not mean that there is no romance in technology. On the contrary, nerds have become sexy gods of hurry; the systems and gadgets they work on are ever-more cunning and wondrous. While there can be heroic justification for the use of these inventions, the inventions don't depend on that morality. They exist to be powerful, in fresh, thrilling, hip ways.

But as these technical means of hurry become established, a kind of familiar speed inflation that has little to do with being fresh and hip sets in. Everyone's pace has to pick up, just to do what have become the ordinary tasks of the day. Cars and interstates mean long commutes are possible and soon common; speedy communications mean people know of more tasks more quickly and have more work to get done in a typical day; news about politics, music, fashion, and celebrity marriages and divorces comes at such a pace that missing a few days can mean missing a whole wave of national emotion. And as technological invention hurries on toward its next amazing product, the hurry to stay in touch, to stay on top of events urges consumers to stay on top of the next innovation. Oddly enough, a kind of heroism reemerges, as in this hurry-driven social life each person wages his or her own great battle to keep up.

This means that attempts to be like gods presently involve fewer dishes of ambrosia and more sophisticated devices like Bluetooth. The superpower racing against the clock these days is technology, and behind that technology stand the businesses that both depend on and create it. The logic of the tools is more and more elegant power, particularly speed, for its own sake, but the aim of its producers is to make a profit by increasing that speed, both in the technological products and in the processes for generating and marketing them.

There is no shame in making a legitimate profit, and the demand for speed in business has had some positive effects, such as the streamlining of management so that workers have better access to design and quality control.[3] The pressure to be creative, bold, and still prudent in the face of obstacles creates its own kind of heroism among businesspeople. But this, again, is distinct from the hurry of Superman or of the BlackBerry. The speed of a corporation is set by the game of competition, not the tragedy of mortality or the aesthetics of efficiency. Profit is made on the margin, and that margin is often a matter of the hours or days or months by which one is ahead of the competition. Time is money: any means of shrinking time spent is a way of shrinking costs, and one way of running a profitable business is simply to get there first. The company, then, that has the best technology may be able to discover new products and markets, communicate findings, and adapt processes more quickly than its competitors. The corollary is that the company that most quickly develops the new fastest technology has itself a winning product, until the next contender comes along. The tools and the work for which they are developed drive each other into further increases in tempo. These hurrying gods do not look back, they do not regret or grieve. They "move forward."[4]

The face of the new god who hurries, in potent confluence of human heroism, the competitive race of business, and the cool factor of technology, is the face of Jack Bauer of the "real-time" thriller *24*. Superman overcame human boundaries because he was not human; Bauer overcomes them through a combination of technology, courage, pragmatism, and a ruthlessness justified by the similarly ruthless ticking of the clock. Season after season, he keeps coming back in ever-more frantic races against evil, because the program sells. Though he is only the latest in a long line of heroes racing against the clock, forcing themselves to abandon every hesitation for the sake of meeting the urgent threat, the logic of hurry works itself out particularly brutally in those plotlines, as even torture seems a necessary element of the heroic rush against evil.

Meanwhile, around the world, away from the glamour of *24*, real soldiers struggle with time. Above all others, soldiers are the ones asked to hurry through every obstacle to finish the job the nation demands. The "rush" of battle can be intoxicating, and it can be horrifying. In its wake comes what can be an unwelcome stillness. The flip side of hurry, the tedium of waiting for the next big push, outlines the heartbreaking truth of what hurry can do to us.

The hurry of heroism, competition, or efficient technology has a moral logic and great power to shape lives. Our habits, both in leisure and in work, in production and in consumption, in imagination and in practice share in these pressures to hurry. Realizing this can help us to understand why in spite of a widespread sense that "slowing down" would be a good thing, most of us find ourselves unable to resist the urge to rush. Among those who most feel this pressure, clergy have earned themselves a special niche. For them, the more general pressures of the culture to hurry are complicated by the eternal import of the ministry. One can never have done enough, never have satisfactorily "made the most" of one's time. The field of studies on burnout among ministers has increased continually since its inception, and our mutually reinforcing heroic stories, structures, and practices of hurry may be the reason.[5] It seems that the problem of competing obligations to family, self, and ministry are tragic and intractable. Faced with this problem, people find tools to give greater speed, but no amount of speeding up and working efficiently can allow ministers to fit it all in. It is the nature of hurry that something must be sacrificed, someone's needs or plans have to be ignored or even run over. But for the minister, how can such a sacrifice be made? Whose needs will get shoved aside? Unbearable stress over trying to meet all such needs sufficiently is simply evidence of a good-faith attempt to do what can never be done.

Yet it is clergy who are charged with leading the public practice of Sabbath-keeping, in the weekly gathering for worship. In an era in which hurrying is the mark of vitality and moral seriousness, what does it mean that it is in the leisure of shared weekly worship, not the hustle of creativity and rescue, that Christians claim most vividly to encounter their God?

God Does Not Hurry

There is one more type of hurrying divine-wanna-be we could add to our list: the revolutionary. Gerhard Lohfink in *Does God Need the Church?* claims that "all revolutionaries have one basic problem: they are all short of time."[6] The task is so urgently necessary, the evil to be overcome so great, that change cannot happen fast enough. Lohfink most likely has in mind the Stalin-era revolutionaries of the Soviet Union who could not tolerate dissent, even of intelligent farmers and engineers who only wanted to do their jobs well or the leaders of the Terror during France's revolutionary years, for whom execution of any who questioned their regime became an exercise in efficiency.

But God's revolutionary work in the world, Lohfink argues, is not of that sort. God allows the lives of creatures to unfold in freedom.

> God, like all revolutionaries, desires the overturning, the radical alteration of the whole society—for in this the revolutionaries are right: what is at stake is the whole world, and the change must be radical, for the misery of the world cries to heaven and it begins deep within the human heart. But how can anyone change the world and society at its roots without taking away freedom?[7]

We may wish, and many have, that God would be less patient. A little "rending of the heavens" seems in order, given the brutality of humans to one another. That's surely what Superman would do. But, whether we like it or not, it is not the way of Israel's God.

The Bible describes creation, for example, in two different stories (Gen. 1–2:3 and Gen. 2:4–25), but neither one depicts any particular rush. Each element of the world appears in its own time, and God stops to admire each. It is not fear or danger, but a fullness of harmony that characterizes God's action. This God is not heroic, because the story is not a tragedy in which the hero could suffer and strive against obstacles. When it is all done, there is no need to plunge right into the next big thing: God is satisfied and rests.

Even with the fall of humanity and the spread of sin, which one might expect to put a bit more urgency into God's approach, we find God watching over generations of humanity before finally acting, to destroy them in the flood (Genesis 3–9). That one great revolutionary move, however, is the exception that proves the rule: God promises after the flood never again to resort to the efficient solution of wiping out sinful humanity. Instead, the story shifts to the work of building trust with one couple and, through them, with one people (Genesis 12–50). God made a covenant with them to be faithful, and the medium of this pledge is time.

The covenant has meaning only because it is faithfulness across time, a faithfulness that does not have its fulfillment immediately. Such a pledge is one of the most difficult and dangerous things a human can do, given the uncertainties of the future, but it is dangerous because it closes off the possibility of hurrying. The covenant partner must endure, must be patient.

For God to act in this way is simply astonishing. God closes off options and commits to patience, resigning the power of immediate satisfaction, in favor of the slow work of building a love. Small wonder biblical writers compare the covenant to a stormy marriage. The nature of the commitment of marriage is that it permits a couple to take their time growing in love. Bad patches are not cause for panic. Nor do warm moments stand on their own, as lovely but singular and therefore unreliable. Covenant faithfulness means God stands with this particular people through good and bad times, coaxing and arguing and reconciling. Over generations, Israel learns that God is faithful, even when Israel is not. God waits.

Grace can move quickly, but it does not hurry. Or to put it another way, God doesn't use force on those he calls. When scripture speaks of God's omnipotence, it is not the power to obliterate those who disobey that is impressive. Obliterating enemies, after all, only proves that their resistance could not be overcome. It is a reaction to a failure of power, an attempt to stem the tide of opposition. As Barth puts it, "Since He has willed to provide us with the sign of Cain and that of Noah, do we not have to say that the omnipotent Godhead of the living God consists only in the fact that He is not impatient but patient?"[8] The fullness of power is not to react heroically against sinners, nor is it to efficiently make a better product than humanity, but to bear with them and to carry on bringing about the salvation of all, undaunted.

In this, Jesus is the full exemplification of God's patience. God does act, in the fullness of time, by sending the Son to live a life, to gestate and be born, to grow and learn, and eventually to suffer injustice and die. Even then, at the moment when grace overturns in a cosmic revolution the laws of eternal justice, the division of God and humanity, even then, God lets it take time. Jesus lay in the tomb Friday night, Saturday, Saturday night . . . and only on the third day was resurrected, out of our sight, so that the heroic moment when the stone was rolled away is one only God witnessed. God, it seems, is content to let things take time.

Jesus himself shows a strange and disturbing patience. According to Mark's version, while on the way to heal Jairus's daughter, who was "at the point of death," (Mark 5:23 NAB) Jesus stops to ask who in the crowd had touched him, and he refuses to go on until he has met and comforted the woman who had been healed. She had not wanted to delay him; she saw that he was a busy man and she thought she could just sneak in her own need unobtrusively, without getting in the way or slowing him down. But Jesus not only does not push the obstacle out of his hurried path; he seeks this woman out and stops for her sake. Surely, Jairus must have been losing his mind at such a delay, and when he found out that they had not made it in time, that his daughter was dead, what grief and rage he might have felt! Precious moments wasted on talking to someone who was already cured had cost his daughter's life. Yet Jesus neither reconciles himself to this tragedy nor, Superman-like, turns back time. He does something new: he raises the girl, with a gentleness both to her and to her family that simply refuses to be rushed. God has time enough for what needs to be, time to be gentle to both the woman in the crowd and to the child in her home. "Do not be afraid; just have faith" (Mark 5:36 NAB).

The story of Jairus's daughter suggests that those who long for God to hurry up and act may not need to sacrifice their passion for justice in order to cultivate a hope that can endure waiting. God's patience is better news than it may appear: "The Lord does not delay his promise, as some regard 'delay,' but he is patient with you, not wishing that any should perish but that all should come to repentance" (2 Peter 3:9 NAB). The story of the wheat and the tares, in which God the farmer refuses to weed until the plants are all full grown, is not about God's lack of interest in the harvest, but about a patience that allows every opportunity for the weeds to turn out to be fruitful and life-giving. This is good news for the weeds, and it ought to be good news to all of us who are not entirely wheatlike. God will not be hurried in the work of loving each one of us, no matter how much we may think hurry is exactly what is needed for the sake of Jairus's daughter . . . or for refugees in Sudan, for millions infected with AIDS, for children around the world dying for lack of clean water. Whether we like it or not, the fact remains: God has all the time in the world, and seems quite ready to use it rather than rush to smite the evildoers.

> Then the LORD answered me and said:
> Write down the vision
> Clearly upon the tablets,
> so that one can read it readily.
> For the vision still has its time,
> presses on to fulfillment, and will not disappoint;
> If it delays, wait for it,
> it will surely come, it will not be late.
> The rash man has no integrity;
> but the just man, because of his faithfulness, shall live.
>
> (Hab. 2: 2–4 NAB)

Being People Whose God Doesn't Hurry

We are a people who hurry: to get through traffic, to keep up with competition, to be sure our kids get every benefit we can manage, to rescue victims of injustice, even just out of habit. Our tools set us a pace that runs us ragged. We long for stillness, for a dewy country morning's walk (nicely depicted in a five-second shot in a commercial, as holding a shot for five seconds feels like a very long stillness on a TV screen). But such stillness is morally suspect as avoidance, and all too often it feels to us, acclimated as we are to rushing toward achievement, as mere dead-time.

God does not hurry. But what does that mean for us? We are not God, and so knowing that God does not hurry is not the same as knowing that we ought never to do so. That would be not only absurd but presumptuous. When the two-year-old wanders into traffic, a bystander might want to hurry to intervene. Nevertheless, knowing that God does not hurry does change things. The meaning of divine power, it turns out, is not in producing a result simply and elegantly as in technological power, or in beating out the competition, or even in the moral passion that overturns all obstacles in a race to defeat mortality. Divine power is a patience that does not fear running out of time.

Recognizing this can, for one thing, help us think about the importance of worship. Praise, confession, supplication, offering, and receiving—these are activities that, by the standards of efficiency, waste time.[9] They are, nevertheless, absolutely essential to the Christian life. It is in our worship that we remember ourselves as citizens of a city that is not dominated by fear and urgency, but by God's patience and plenty. It can take some time to remember that, given that so much in our lives is about the need to hurry. In this sense, worship is no waste at all, because it is essential to our right understanding of time. Time is the medium across which we receive God's gifts, in word and Eucharist, and in which we by grace are able to offer gifts in return: our praise, our love, and, in union with our brother Jesus, our own lives. A sale is about achieving a result, an exchange of goods, and can be done in a hurry, but the giving of gifts, because it is about mutual love, can't be rushed. In worship, as in other gift giving, we have to have time to look in each other's eyes. Worship is testimony that our efficiency, our excellence, and even our heroism are superseded by the gracious gift of delighted communal rest in God.

The monastic life, because it is so structured around worship, can serve as a testing ground for what the life of people whose God does not hurry might be. It is worth recalling that the clock was invented not to keep track of our work, but to remind monastic communities to stop work and turn to prayer repeatedly during the day.[10] Rather than marking every moment as an identical and scarce commodity to be sold or invested or else lost, the monastic schedule marks time as the unfolding of God's patience, graciously given as space for humans to rejoice in God's goodness. The tools invented within that life serve not to maximize speed or power, but as aids to worship. Work and business, similarly, can be part of a life defined by worship rather than by a race against the clock, as they are defined by meeting human need rather than by competition for scarce resources or new markets. Even the impulse of heroism, the longing to sacrifice oneself for love of others, also becomes an unhurried affair in the monastery: a whole life can be spent in menial labor, in prayer, in solitude and community, as a daily gift of love, renewed by God's own grace, time and again.

That sounds lovely and leisurely, but learning to live time as time-for-worship takes strenuous practice. In Israel's stories of the desert, one of the key tropes is the struggle to learn Sabbath-keeping, and the reason people had trouble learning to rest is that they had to learn to trust God. Coming out of slavery, they were accustomed to fear and scarcity. Learning to live in confident trust took some training, and the story tells us God put them on a strict trust diet. Manna was given only on six days, and on the seventh the people were to rest and eat the extra from the sixth day. God did not teach them to rest after they were secure in their land. Rather, they learned to rest when they were at their most vulnerable. God taught them to trust in someone else's care. The point of Sabbath is not to become more able to go back to work or to take a reward for work well done. The point is that trust in God's care is more fundamental than work. The manna will be given because God is faithful, and our work and rest follow upon the gift. In this sense, human patience is an act of humility as well as trust. The only way we can be patient in a world of danger is by knowing that it is God's gift and not our control that will save the day.

That kind of trust seems obsolete in an economy that provides for those who can pay for food from around the world, fuel to run cars and heat houses, plentiful clothing, and entertainment. But actually, the idea that even in postindustrial society people could be self-sufficient is badly mistaken. That thinking depends in the first place on the assumption that childhood, sickness, and old age are times of frustration, of a lack of full humanity, not moments at which we see most clearly who we really are. In these periods when people are dependent on others and when vulnerability is exposed, they and their caretakers may enter more fully into relationships with others and with God. For those who investigate the plentiful providence of the global economy more carefully, it also becomes clear that this is not a structure based on strong and independent individuals capable of acting on their own. It is a network of relations, some constructive, many abusive, in which we very much are each other's keepers, whether we like it or not. Recognizing our vulnerability and interdependence is a way into seeing our waiting on one another not as a nuisance or an obstacle, but as intrinsic to being the people God created. In patience, we learn to listen and to see more deeply what hurry rushes past—the gifts of God in ourselves, in creation, in one another.

One model of this kind of fruitful patience is the witness of L'Arche communities, where people of varied abilities and disabilities live together in committed, interdependent relations. L'Arche moves at a pace suitable to community, where people accept each other (and themselves), with strengths and weaknesses, admirable and not-so-admirable qualities, and learn how to live together. Core community members, the permanent residents, bear with the assistants, who often arrive unaccustomed to such a pace of life, and in their shared household, they practice hospitality, not for the sake of "fixing" disabilities, but as part of a much deeper change, a shift toward patience.[11]

Humility, trust, patience: none of these virtues, as fine as they are, mean that our world is not full of suffering and injustice, and practicing them is not about denying or insulating oneself from danger and pain. On the contrary, these are virtues that make us more aware of one another's real suffering and more aware simply of one another, as persons rather than statistics or types. It is in patience that we can attempt to fulfill the command not only to love neighbor, but to love our enemies. The efficient solutions—running away or blowing them up—are ruled out. The great icon of God's patience, the cross, is a sobering reminder that giving up hurry, bearing with ourselves and others patiently, is not all about sunsets on quiet beaches. But even the cross and its hours of forced immobility belong to God. There is no God-forsaken place or time. When, in the stillness of not-hurrying we face what we have feared and dodged and run from before, the humble trust that underpins patience can cling to this: God has claimed this place too.

Patience, however, can be easily discredited, because it can so easily be a cover for complacency and cowardice. In 1963, during his own enforced patience in a jail cell in Birmingham, Martin Luther King Jr. wrote a letter in response to a public statement by eight moderate white clergymen. Regarding civil rights demonstrations in Birmingham, the white leaders, Protestant, Catholic, and Jewish, wrote, "We recognize the natural impatience of people who feel that their hopes are slow in being realized. But we are convinced that these demonstrations are unwise and untimely."[12] King responded, famously, with a defense of impatience: "Frankly, I have yet to engage in a direct-action campaign that was 'well timed' in the view of those who have not suffered unduly from the disease of segregation. For years now I have heard the word 'Wait!' It rings in the ear of every Negro with piercing familiarity. This 'Wait' has almost always meant 'Never.' We must come to see, with one of our distinguished jurists, that 'justice too long delayed is justice denied.'"[13]

King was right to condemn this call for passivity masquerading as a call for patience. For those who live in God's patience, this distinction between patience and passivity is particularly necessary. Passivity in the face of sin is not patience, but despair. Patience, rooted in a sense of living in God's world, faces sin without panic, without the heedlessness of hurry. Karl Barth is said to have commented, facing the rise of Nazism in 1933, "We must go on as though nothing has happened." He did not mean that they should do nothing, but that they must not be intimidated into reaction or be dissuaded from any good work they had under way, whether in prayer, study, or charity. Patience is a refusal to allow the opponent to define one's role. In this sense, true patience was at the heart of the civil rights movement, as people endured vicious attacks without allowing themselves and their responses to be defined by them. Their patience, embraced as a matter of their dignity and identity as people of God, allowed them not to strike back. Such patience is no passivity, but a courageous witness to truth.

Patience, like any virtue, is governed by prudence, and among Christians, even prudence has charity as its backbone. To advocate patience, then, has to mean advocating a patience that is not evasion but is exercised in keeping with love of God and neighbor. The lives and deaths of the Trappist monks of the Monastery of Notre Dame of Atlas of Tibhirine, in Algeria, exemplify that kind of patience. When threatened by extremists, they carefully considered their options—to leave Algeria altogether, to move to a safer location within Algeria, to remain in their place but with armed guards around them, or to remain as they had been. Their neighbors, though recognizing the danger, asked them to remain. If they left, they would be giving the extremists what they wanted, thereby strengthening them. For the brothers, who had spent their lives witnessing peacefully to God's generosity and gladly finding friends and fellow lovers of God among their Muslim neighbors, this argument was persuasive. They also thought it would be contrary to their calling to depend upon armed guards for their safety. So they remained, as they had been, living in their monastery and praying the liturgy of the hours, welcoming anyone who came to them unarmed.

They knew that in this act of patience they were risking their lives. Patience was not a way of avoiding or of resigning themselves to sin, but a way of abiding faithfully; it was not the necessary skill for surviving without trust, but the way of embodying trust in their calling. Patience was their refusal to be swayed from love.

On the night of March 26–27, 1996, the brothers were kidnapped and on May 21 they were beheaded by their captors. In a letter to his family to be opened after his death, the prior of the community, Father Christian de Chergé, spoke with the voice of patience based in trust in a God whose love is greater than our injustice:

> Obviously, my death will appear to confirm those who hastily judged me naive or idealistic: "Let him tell us now what he thinks of his ideals!" But these persons should know that finally my most avid curiosity will be set free. This is what I shall be able to do, God willing: immerse my gaze in that of the Father to contemplate with him His children of Islam just as He sees them, all shining with the glory of Christ, the fruit of His Passion, filled with the Gift of the Spirit whose secret joy will always be to establish communion and restore the likeness, playing with the differences. For this life lost, totally mine and totally theirs, I thank God, who seems to have willed it entirely for the sake of that JOY in everything and in spite of everything. In this THANK YOU, which is said for everything in my life from now on, I certainly include you, friends of yesterday and today, and you, my friends of this place, along with my mother and father, my sisters and brothers and their families—you are the hundredfold granted as was promised! And also you, my last-minute friend, who will not have known what you were

doing: Yes, I want this THANK YOU and this GOODBYE to be a "GOD BLESS" for you, too, because in God's face I see yours. May we meet again as happy thieves in Paradise, if it please God, the Father of us both.[14]

Conclusion

We may need to hurry sometimes, because, for example, buildings do catch fire. And if knowing that every day thousands die for lack of clean water leaves us with no sense of urgency, then we have surely not yet known anything about God's love. But recalling that God's patience with us is the first and essential truth of the gift of time can save us from coming to hate those who are obstacles to us as well as coming to hate all in ourselves that is an obstacle. In families where parents and children and spouses bear with one another, in neighborhoods where people know one another well enough to be able to offer support in times of trouble, in schools where a student's learning matters more than the hoop to be jumped on time at the end of the year: our lives are full of places to practice and celebrate the beauty of lives unfolding across God's gift of time. These are not domestic or emotional backwaters. These are places where the truth of the creation is being lived. Courage, ingenuity, and productivity all find their place too, working in God's good time rather than against it.

In a beautiful reflection on time, Tolkien wrote of creation as a work of music, a theme declared by the creator, Ilúvatar, and sung by the angels in their many voices. They

> began to fashion the theme of Ilúvatar to a great music; and a sound arose of endless interchanging melodies woven in harmony that passed beyond hearing into the depths and into the heights, and the places of the dwelling of Ilúvatar were filled to overflowing, and the music and the echo of the music went out into the Void, and it was not void.[15]

The gift of time is musical, moving at a pace that is fluid but ordered, growing to fullness without racing to get finished. The beat may be fast or slow, but the good musician knows not to hurry. Time is not the enemy, something to be gotten through; it is tempo, carrying mobile harmonies. Although sin enters in through one angel who wants to win glory by introducing his own themes, Ilúvatar continues to weave the music through to its end, not silencing the discordant elements, but introducing a new theme,

> . . . and it was unlike the others. For it seemed at first soft and sweet, a mere rippling of gentle sounds in delicate melodies; but it could not be quenched, and it took to itself power and profundity.[16]

As the unharmonious "loud, and vain, and endlessly repeated" music of sin strove to overcome this new music, "it seemed that its most triumphant notes were taken by the other and woven into its own solemn pattern."[17]

The braying of injustice and vanity may drive us to abandon the musical pace of time in favor of more efficient destruction of such disorder. But God does not despair, and humility demands that if God has not given up, neither should humans. Our part is to listen in the unfolding of time for God's music, and to accept the invitation to join our voices to it.

When this struggle makes us weary, and it does, it is encouraging to remember that Jesus does actually tell a story about God hurrying: a loving father, despised and rejected by his son, waits years for the faithless child to return. As soon as his patience is rewarded with the sight of that prodigal on the road home, then God hurries, casting all caution to the wind, racing out to meet this lost child. The love that waits, scandalous in its patience, will finally be unreserved in its haste to welcome us into the feast of reconciliation. In the meantime, we wait in joyful hope.[18]

God Does Not Want to Write Your Love Story

Margaret Kim Peterson and Dwight N. Peterson

For the past number of years we have been teaching a senior-level college course called Christian Marriage. As we have done so, we have noticed that a large proportion of our students, while professing (sincerely, we believe) a desire for unambiguously Christian things like love and marriage, are at the same time in the grip of a powerfully seductive fantasy in which the two main characters are Cinderella and Prince Charming. The drama is all about "falling in love" and the action consists primarily in an elaborate wedding followed by a ride into the sunset.

This fantasy is not limited to our students. There exists a small avalanche of books written by Christian young people for other Christian young people, in which the authors relate their own stories of romance and advise their readers how they too can find their prince or princess and live happily ever after. Our students own shelves of these books and recommend them to us, and it was while reading one such volume, entitled *When God Writes Your Love Story*, that it began to dawn on us with particular clarity how different these stories of romance are from any traditionally Christian understanding of marriage.[1]

In short, as we have put it ever since to our students, God does *not* want to write your love story. In saying this, we do not mean to imply that God has no interest in your love life. God cares about whom people love and how they love them, even as God cares about every other aspect of our lives. We are also not meaning to be specifically critical of any one author or book. The theme of the "love story" is common to a great deal of Christian writing about love and marriage, and it is the entire genre that is problematic. It embodies a very specific vision of what counts as a "love story" and of how love stories are to be pursued, one that in our judgment is at best sub-Christian.

This is, of course, far from the intention of the authors of Christian romantic-advice books. Many of these authors are perceptive observers of the contemporary social and relational scene and of the loneliness and destructiveness that too often characterize that environment and the lives of the young people who find themselves enmeshed in it. These authors' stated aim is to offer an alternative to the world of hook-ups and breakups, an alternative that is wholesome and satisfying and that speaks to their readers' longings for intimacy and a shared sense of purpose. And they mean for that alternative to be distinctively Christian; they mean to point the way, not just to any love story, but to a love story such as God himself might write.

We don't think it works out that way. The ideal of the "love story," as it is described and promoted in Christian romantic-advice books, seems to us as deeply problematic as the undeniably destructive patterns of relationship and non-relationship it is meant to replace. Both in substance (what is a love story?) and in strategy (what should you do in order to have one?), the romantic ideal of the love story owes far less to the gospel than it does to Disneyland and Madison Avenue. Indeed, it is its affinity with broader cultural ideals of individualism and consumerism that gives the fantasy of romance much of its power over the American imagination, including the American Christian imagination.

So what exactly is the fantasy of romance? What are the strategies that romantic-advice books recommend as means for achieving this fantasy? And what alternatives to this fantasy and these strategies might the gospel of Christ crucified and risen have to offer, alternatives that might, in fact, answer more adequately the very real and intensely felt longings for love and relationship that characterize the lives of so many of our students and their peers?

Hook-up Culture and Its Christian Equivalent

Let's begin where the romantic-advice books tend to begin, with a look at the contemporary social and relational landscape inhabited by many young people today. When we began teaching our Christian Marriage course, a term current among our students was "friends with benefits." As semi-clueless members of an older generation, we had to have this explained to us: it meant, our students told us, the practice of having sexual relations, or the next thing to them, with people with whom one was otherwise "just friends."

Ripples of embarrassed giggles spread over the lecture hall as our students educated us on this topic, which was, it appeared, foreign to no one, although the degree of students' personal involvement in such activities varied considerably. It didn't seem so funny the next week, when one of our students showed up in class with eyes swollen from weeping, on the verge of yet more tears: her much-adored younger brother, who was still in high school, had the night before disclosed to her and to their parents not only that he had gotten a girl pregnant, but that the relationship in the context of which this pregnancy had occurred was not even one of particular intimacy. They were just "friends with benefits."

The notion of "friends with benefits" now seems positively quaint. It has been replaced by the hook-up culture, in which one has sexual relations, or the next thing to them, with perfect strangers. This phenomenon is described in books like *Unhooked*, which focuses on how sexual activity among high-school and college-age young women is increasingly decoupled from anything resembling intimate relationship.[2] It should perhaps go without saying that, among heterosexuals at least, the involvement of men in the hook-up culture is just as great as that of women, although it is possible that the effects of that culture on men may be different in detail from its effects on women.

It is difficult to believe, however, that the hook-up culture is anything but bad for everyone, male and female. The more casual sexual behavior becomes, the less it serves to deepen existing intimacy, and the more it becomes a substitute for and even an impediment to intimacy. After all, if you begin by falling into bed with someone, what could you possibly gain by getting to know him or her afterward? And the pleasures and costs of hooking up turn out to be rather like those of pornography: the pleasure is increasingly fleeting and shallow, and the costs come due eventually, in the guise of a corroded and misshapen capacity for genuine relationship with anyone.

It is no wonder, then, that the authors of Christian romantic-advice books take so dim a view of the contemporary social scene, and why their books find a ready audience among Christian young people, who see in themselves and in others the damage wrought by unwise sexual involvement and who long for something better. But before we consider what that something better might be, we would do well to reflect for a moment on ways in which contemporary Christian culture inadvertently contributes to and participates in the world of the hook-up.

Make no mistake about it: Christians are part of this phenomenon. They are part of it in the very straightforward sense that a good many Christian young people are not simply scandalized observers of the hook-up culture but are themselves participants in it. Again the analogy with pornography is pertinent. Business analysts have shown that in hotel rooms in which pay-per-view porn is available (and that is now the case in the majority of mid-level to high-end hotels), more than half of all guests pay to view the porn.[3] The use of pornography, in other words, has become more common than not.

And so it is with casual sexual behavior among young people like those in our Christian Marriage class. Among our students there are, of course, some who have lived very chastely. But there are not a few at the opposite end of the spectrum, and the majority are somewhere in the middle, behaving in ways that their elders would undoubtedly find shockingly loose but that in their own social milieu are so common as to seem almost inevitable.

This seeming inevitability of casual and otherwise nonmarital sexual behavior is a sad indictment of the Christian formation that contemporary Christian young people are receiving—or not receiving—in their churches and in their homes. What is typically absent from that formation is any attempt to grapple in truthful and theologically substantive ways with contemporary social realities. The result is young people who may know what the rules are, but who are unable to think of any persuasive reason to obey them.

This phenomenon was illustrated for us vividly by a student who asked, half sheepishly, half defiantly, if we could explain to her precisely why she should not move in with her boyfriend upon graduation. "I know it's wrong," she said, "but everybody does it, and it would be so much more convenient. And if we don't live together officially, he'll end up spending the night anyway. Why should we go to the trouble and expense of setting up two separate apartments? Who would we think we were kidding?"

Along with the absence of creative theological engagement with contemporary realities, there is typically present in much Christian rhetoric about sex a great deal of emphasis on virginity and on "waiting." But here again the result too often is not to counter cultural mores regarding sexual behavior, but rather inadvertently to reinforce them. Talking about sex primarily as something to be waited for encourages a passivity in young people that tends not to be able to withstand the tug of broader cultural forces. It also encourages the equation of sexual maturity with sexual activity. Mature manhood and womanhood are not presented as states people have the opportunity to grow into gradually, whether or not they ever marry or engage in sexual relations. The assumption appears rather to be that one will remain a child until he or she begins having sex, and that Christians ought to wait until they are married both for sex and for adult status.

It is unsurprising, therefore, that many Christian young people resent being shunted into singles groups that seem to function as holding pens for those who are not yet allowed to join the grown-ups, and equally unsurprising that many of them do not, in fact, "wait for marriage." In a society fraught with divorce and in which the securing of a marriage partner is exclusively the responsibility of the individual, marriage can seem impossibly distant and risky. Sex, on the other hand, is readily available, whether with someone you know or with someone you don't. So why wait for marriage, when you can have the benefits of sex right now?

There is another more subtle way in which contemporary Christian attitudes toward sex and commitment mirror rather than contrast with those of society at large. Part of the appeal of the hook-up culture is that it offers the pleasure of sex without the danger of commitment. Commitment is dangerous, so the thought goes, partly because of the possibility of a breakup, but also because commitment limits one's options. A person who is sincerely attached to a boyfriend or girlfriend might allow that relationship to influence decisions about education or career, and might as a result not succeed or achieve as much as he or she might have otherwise. It is permissible, therefore, to pursue sex, but love must at all costs be delayed, lest some premature commitment derail one's life or career.

Counterintuitive though it may seem, there are many contemporary Christians who share this sense that if young people get too tied down too soon, that's bad. The difference is only in what is seen as too tied down. The hook-up culture sees any relationship at all as too tied down. What is left of the dating culture sees early marriage as too tied down. The Christian culture sees parenthood as too tied down. If young people want to have sex, they can get married, but they mustn't have babies until they are "ready." What counts as "ready" varies: done with college, done with graduate school, established in a career, financially secure, perhaps just simply older than they are now. Most fundamentally, they need to be in a place in which having a child will not unduly restrict their options.

Most of our students are not married, but in the lives of nearly every one who is, we see evidence of this deep cultural bias against young parenthood. There are the young husbands and wives who long for a baby but say they feel they must wait because their parents, while delighted with their marriage, would be horrified if they got pregnant. There are the married women who are terrified that they might become pregnant, because, they say, it would be disastrous if they did. The women who do conceive, or the men whose wives become pregnant, typically view the event with dismay: there were so many things they wanted to do before they had children, and now they won't be able to do them.

And then there is the story told by a student whose close friend, still in her early twenties, had a baby at some respectable interval after being married. The friend had described, with some bitterness, her sense that the people around her disapproved of her young married motherhood more than they disapproved even of unwed motherhood. After all, an unwed mother could be patronizingly dismissed as having made a mistake, whereas she, a married woman, had evidently done this on purpose.

What a good many contemporary Christians seem to have lost sight of is that Christians have traditionally understood marriage, sex, and children as things that properly go together. Marriages are meant to be fruitful, and in the absence of modern contraceptive methods, most marriages are, and in fairly short order. But we live in a contraceptive culture, one in which the good baby is a responsibly planned baby, and whose appearance on the scene is the result of a completely different set of decisions from the decision to get married.

The result too often is Christians who see marriage as a church-sanctioned form of romance. Marriage, in this view, makes sex respectable. But married sex is not supposed to result in babies any more than unmarried sex is, at least not until the young couple are not so young any more. Why not? Well, because young love is supposed to be unfettered and carefree; it is supposed to be characterized by romantic getaways and lacy lingerie, not by night feedings and decisions whether to use cloth or disposable diapers.

And in this exaltation of romance, understood as something quite separate from—and indeed likely to be impaired by—parenthood, too many Christians come perilously close to endorsing an ideal of relationship that differs only in the presence of a wedding ring from the ideal of relationship found in the broader culture. Get married, Christian parents and relationship advisers urge Christian young people, but when you get married, be sure that what you are getting is a love story, a romance that fulfills your desires for intimacy while leaving you free to pursue whatever other goals you may have. And whatever you do, don't get pregnant on your honeymoon!

The "Perfect Love Story"

So what is the love story that the authors of Christian romantic-advice books would have their readers aspire to? In a word, it is perfect: it is the perfect embodiment of romance itself, the apotheosis of every chick flick ever made, a kind of fairy tale on steroids. It is, in the words of a song by one Christian romantic-advice giver, "the kind of perfect love story that I have always dreamed would somehow come into my life."[4]

In the Perfect Love Story, no compromises are ever made. No one settles for less than he or she deserves, and everyone deserves only the best. She is beautiful; he is handsome. She is thin; he is muscular. She plays the piano; he plays the guitar. Both parties embody every item on the other's list of desirable qualities in a spouse, a list that each of them has been keeping since he or she was twelve.

The Perfect Love Story is dramatic. When she first catches sight of him, she thinks, "Wow!" When his eyes first meet hers, sparks fly. Their developing relationship is filled with romantic dinners for two, exchanges of thoughtful little gifts, maybe a short-term mission trip to an exotic locale. He and she are at center stage all of the time, since, after all, they are the stars. His proposal is creative and personal and romantic; it is the kind of story that is bound to circulate among their friends and family for years to come.

The Perfect Love Story is smooth sailing. Everyone is healthy; everyone's family is pious and untroubled and supportive. The couple themselves are unambiguously happy all of the time. If conflicts or hurt feelings related to past romantic or sexual entanglements arise, these are dealt with in the space of ten or fifteen minutes at most. Otherwise, the couple never fights, because they have God at the center of their relationship, they are clear about their biblical roles as a man and as a woman, and, after all, they love each other.

In the Perfect Love Story, there is always plenty of money. Flowers, candlelit dinners, and extravagant gestures abound, showing the world that he loves her. On Valentine's Day in particular, all these things, plus chocolate, are an absolute necessity. Any woman who is offered less is justified in feeling herself severely wronged, and any woman who would settle for less is likely to be chastised by her friends for not holding out for more. And when the proposal comes along, no woman in a perfect love story is ever offered, or would think of accepting, an engagement ring with a diamond of less than a full carat weight.

The Perfect Love Story finds its proper climax in a perfect wedding, which is necessarily an elaborate affair. The complexity of planning such a wedding is offset somewhat by the fact that the bride has been planning it since before she met the groom; in fact, planning her wedding was a required senior project at the private Christian high school she attended. Of course, the wedding is expensive; the bride's friends must spend a small fortune for the privilege of being bridesmaids, but they are presumed willing to do this, because, after all, a perfect love story deserves a perfect wedding.

In the wedding ceremony, the friends of the bride and groom testify to the fairy-tale nature of the bridal couple's romance. In his sermon, the minister does the same. At the reception, the bride and groom are introduced as the prince and princess of the day, and at the close of the festivities they are borne off to the airport for the start of a honeymoon in a remote and sunny location, ready to embrace the blissful and cloudless future that God prepares for those who wait on him.

We are not making any of this up. Everything we have said about the Perfect Love Story is something that our students have told us that they expect or want in a relationship, or that they have been taught they should expect or want in a relationship. A good many of these things we have found explicitly stated in one Christian relationship-advice book or another. And these books are very clear: this is all of God. God is the author of romance, and if you allow God to shape your destiny, a perfect love story is bound to be your reward, whether in this life or in eternity.

We don't believe it. It should go without saying how profoundly unrealistic all of this is. People are not perfect, and their love stories are not perfect. They are not all conventionally attractive. More often than not they are strapped for cash and burdened with debt. They do in fact experience conflict in their relationships, conflict that no amount of recourse to pious clichés or "biblical" gender roles can wish away. Their experiences as members of their families and as individuals are always mixed, and sometimes the rivers of sorrow run deep indeed.

Given the undeniable obviousness of these realities, it should be easy to see that the perfect love story is at best a kind of escapist fantasy. But fantasies do not exist in a realm of pure imagination; they have a way of shaping the practical imagination, the hopes and plans and decisions of the people who hold them. And in our observation, the fantasy of romance shapes the imagination of Christian young people in ways that are narrow and shallow and fundamentally un-Christian.

The fantasy of romance is narrow in its exclusive focus on one person, that perfect partner with whom alone all one's desires for intimacy and love will finally be fulfilled. It is assumed that romance is the only kind of love that actually counts as love, and that the person who has not met his or her "one true love" has yet to experience either intimacy or happiness. The single person is lonely by definition; no matter how many friends or family members that person may have, he or she is not married and is therefore alone in the world.

A practical result of this monomaniacal focus on "the one" is the reluctance often felt by Christian young people to devote themselves to developing meaningful relationships with anyone they do not view as a marriage prospect. Friendships with single persons of the opposite sex are seen as dangerous (what if you fall into sin?), and friendships with anyone else are seen as beside the point (since romance is by definition the only source of intimacy). The presumptive loneliness of the single person ends up becoming a self-fulfilling prophecy.

The fantasy of romance is shallow, in that it does not involve any substantive reflection on cultural ideals of love. It simply assumes that what we see in the movies is love, true love, and that this is therefore identical with the love that God has for believers and that God desires believers to have for one another. Ancient Christian language about the church as the bride of Christ and God as lover of the soul is interpreted through the rose-tinted lenses of contemporary ideals of romance, and the results are by turns pathetic, comic, and grotesque.

One Christian romantic-advice book cites as an inspiring example a woman who describes her singleness in these terms: "Right now, I'm just learning to be God's princess."[5] Not long after we read this, one of our students, a pastor's son, told us of an engaged couple who had approached his father to ask if he would conduct their wedding ceremony. Their plan, they told him, was for the bride and groom to dress as Snow White and her prince, and for the groomsmen to come dressed as the seven dwarves. It is a short step, evidently, from being God's princess to being a Disney princess.

And then there were the posters that appeared one Valentine's Day, tacked on bulletin boards all over campus: "Single? Don't worry—you are the bride of Christ!" These words were accompanied by an illustration of a heart pierced with a cross and dripping with blood. We suspect these posters were put up by a well-meaning encourager of the lovelorn whose theological and cultural muddle-headedness caused him or her to fail to recognize these words and image as an offensive parody of the Sacred Heart of Jesus, and instead to present them as a Valentine's Day pep talk for those into whose life God has not yet brought "the one."

Most significantly, the fantasy of romance is rooted in a story different from the Christian one. The fantasy of romance assumes that the fundamental human problem is loneliness, and prescribes romantic love as the remedy. Once you meet and marry "the one," your problems are solved. You are perfect, your partner is perfect, your relationship is perfect, all the two of you need from one another is "intimacy," and the two of you together stand in no need of anything else from anyone else. Romance has saved you both out of your single loneliness and launched you into a future in which you have no needs that are not already fulfilled by each other.

The Christian story starts from what seems a similar place: the alienation of people from one another and from God. But in a Christian understanding, the human predicament goes far deeper than the loneliness felt by a dateless college student on a Saturday night, and the remedy goes much further than the provision of matchmaking services to the pious. Charles Wesley, in his hymn *Jesus, Lover of My Soul*, suggests a few aspects of human neediness and the remedies with which God in Christ meets those needs: sin with forgiveness, death with life, sickness with healing, weakness with strength, faintheartedness with encouragement, defenselessness with protection, despair with hope.[6]

What he does not mention in this hymn is either singleness or marriage (one or both of which would undoubtedly be the subject of a hymn of this title, were it to be written today). The Christian tradition simply has never seen singleness as among the fundamental problems of humanity, or marriage as among the primary benefits of redemption. Indeed, there have been seasons in the church's life in which it has been difficult for Christians to see the positive value that marriage does have in the economy of God. In certain sectors of the contemporary church, however, it seems that the pendulum has swung to the other extreme, with marriage viewed as the central means by which people are saved out of what would otherwise be a life of unbearable alienation.

It is thus profoundly ironic that the lens through which many modern Christians have come to interpret marriage, the fantasy of romance, turns out to be so splintering and isolating a phenomenon. Romance, through its exclusive focus on the one true love, ends up separating people two by two from any other substantive human relationship. And as the sociologists tell us, it is in part that very separation from supportive networks of friends and family that makes many modern marriages as brittle and prone to collapse as they are.

It might be that what contemporary Christians need is less romance and more love. Christian love is unitive and community-forming; it weaves people together into familial and churchly networks of mutual care and dependence on one another and on God. Husbands and wives, neighbors and friends, children and grandchildren, widows and orphans, all are adopted by God into the household of the church and invited to love and care for one another in ways that certainly include the bond of marriage but also include a range of other human relationships, all of which involve real connection, real intimacy, real enjoyment of other people, a real participation in the redemptive work of God in the world.

Romantic Fantasies and the Quest
for the Perfect Partner

When we first began teaching our Christian Marriage class, we were puzzled by the number of students who, in describing their relationship status, would tell us that they were single and then tell us how long they had been single: two months, two years, all their lives. Eventually we realized that what they meant was that for that period of time they had not been dating anyone. We found ourselves having to point out to the class that, speaking legally and theologically, the alternative to singleness is not "dating," but marriage.

Speaking experientially, however, dating is the defining emotional experience in the lives of many young people like our students. This is so particularly in more conservative social and religious settings where the utter anomie of the hook-up culture has not yet taken hold. Adolescence has become for many a time of constant cycling in and out of temporarily exclusive dating relationships, each of which is characterized by intense emotional—and sometimes physical—attachment and followed, when it ends, by intense disappointment, disillusionment, and despair.

The fact is that as pleasant as the experience of falling in love may be, falling out of love is considerably less pleasant. And as painful as it may be to find that one wants out of a romantic relationship, it is even more painful to find that it is one's partner who wants out. The authors of Christian romantic-advice books are well aware of this; indeed, in many instances they have learned their lesson the hard way. And so when they hold out to their readers the fantasy of the perfect love story, they hold out with the other hand a strategy for securing such a love story that does not bring with it the risks and potential disappointments of the dating scene.

Thwarted romance is so painful, say these authors, not because there is anything wrong with romance as an ideal, but because people pursue romance the wrong way. Young people date anyone they happen to fancy; they become emotionally attached to people they would never dream of marrying, and then suffer the consequences when those ill-advised relationships break up. They are trying to write their own love stories, and they are not good at it. They need to stop trusting themselves and start trusting God. They need to let go and let God write their love stories.

To let God write your love story means that you refrain from pursuing a romantic relationship with anyone unless and until God reveals to you that a particular person is "the one," the perfect partner whom God has been preparing for you from before the foundation of the world. God wants romance for you, and in God's own time he will provide the perfect partner. Until then, the pious Christian will watch and wait and hope and not date.

How exactly does this work? We have read the books on our Christian romantic-advice shelf very carefully, and the plan seems to be as follows. First, you isolate yourself from any deeply intimate emotional attachment to anyone other than God. Second, you imagine in detail what your future partner is like and what your relationship with him or her will be. And third, when God does bring that special someone into your life, you recognize this person as your future mate through a kind of spiritual intuition that can be summed up in three words: "You just know."

The appeal of the first piece of this advice, the isolation of the self from emotional attachment to others, is that it holds out the promise that one will not suffer the disappointment and pain that come with broken relationships. If you don't get close, you can't get hurt. This is not uncommon advice in Christian circles, even apart from discussions of love and marriage: people are fallible, and they will let you down, but God will never let you down. So don't trust in people; trust only in God.

To a generation of young people growing up ever-more isolated from substantive relationships with their family members due to the combined effects of ever-longer working hours, ever-fewer family meals, and computers and televisions in every room of the house, this sounds like simple realism. If you are going to have emotional intimacy, it is going to have to be with God alone.

Yet people do long for emotional intimacy with other human beings. In the world of Christian romantic advice, this longing is precisely the same as the longing for marriage. Intimacy is by definition romantic, and people are allowed exactly two intimate relationships in their lives: the first with God, the second with the (future) spouse. In fact, emotional intimacy with anyone other than one's spouse constitutes unfaithfulness to the spouse. Just as Christians should save themselves physically for marriage by remaining sexually pure, so they should save themselves emotionally for marriage by not giving away pieces of their hearts to random boyfriends or girlfriends.

Whatever the problems with the dating scene—and they are many—this is hardly an improvement. Intimacy is not identical with romance, and marital love is not so different from other human loves that one cannot practice on one's parents, siblings, neighbors, and friends. On the contrary: one learns to love precisely by loving and by being loved. The person who has refused on principle to know and to be deeply known by anyone other than God and the hypothetical future spouse is likely to find the marital-intimacy learning curve steep indeed.

The second recommendation offered to seekers of Christian romance—that they form a detailed imaginary portrait of what they are looking for in a spouse and in a marriage—is often accompanied by a concrete suggestion to write it all down, in lists of desiderata and in letters to the future object of your affections. The point of doing so is threefold. First, it will help keep your romantic standards as high as God's are, thus preventing you from settling for less than you want and deserve in a mate. Second, it will give you something to do on romantic occasions like Valentine's Day; instead of being depressed because you have not yet met "the one," you can instead write love letters to him or her. And third, the accumulated cache of lists and letters can be presented to your future spouse on your wedding night as evidence of your premarital faithfulness. You did not spend your single years loving other people but instead were busy looking forward to a life of bliss with your as-yet-unknown mate.

It is, of course, not a good idea for anyone to "settle" in the sense of consenting to marry a person of poor character. So much the better if making lists of qualities desirable in a spouse makes someone less likely to do so. And it is only natural that anyone who hopes to marry should have some idea of what he or she would like to find in a marriage partner; should he or she choose to write those ideas down, there is likely no harm done. That said, we are inclined to see all this detailed fantasizing about an as-yet-to-be-identified future partner as more harmful than beneficial.

Lists of desirable characteristics easily turn into ideals of manhood or womanhood or (in their more spiritualized versions) "Christlikeness." But Jesus is not available as a marriage partner, and neither is any ideal man or woman. There are only particular men and women, each of them far more interesting in his or her particularity than any abstract ideal, but none of them precisely identical with that ideal. The longer your list of nonnegotiable sought-after abstract qualities, the less likely it is that you will be able to bring yourself fully to enjoy and admire and receive as God's gift any of the particular people you happen to meet.

Devoting the Valentine's Days of one's singleness to writing letters to one's future beloved simply concedes far too much to the culture of romance; it constitutes a direct affirmation that Cupid makes the world go round, and that the number one job of anyone not currently attached is to wish he or she were. As for the practice of bestowing shoeboxes full of letters upon one's newly wedded husband or wife—well, this is a heavy burden indeed to impose on one's spouse: "Here are all the fantasies I have ever had about you; now fulfill them."

The third step in letting God write your love story involves the intuitive recognition of someone you do not yet know very well as "the one." Somewhere deep inside yourself, in a place to which only you have access, and in a way that makes it impossible to describe or explain to anyone else the grounds of your confidence, you just know that this is the future spouse whom God has chosen for you. You are thus liberated and empowered to pursue a romantic relationship with him or her.

The insistence of romantic-advice authors on the ineffability of this certainty mirrors the tendency in broad swaths of Christian culture to believe that the less able one is to put things into words, the more deeply one must feel those things. This is so where prayer is concerned, with traditional set forms ("Almighty God, unto whom all hearts are open, all desires known, and from whom no secrets are hid, cleanse the thoughts of our hearts by the inspiration of thy Holy Spirit, that we may perfectly love thee and worthily magnify thy holy name, through Christ our Lord, Amen") suspected of shallowness and insincerity and rejected in favor of contemporary praise-service-style prayer ("Father God, we just want to praise you, um, Father God . . ."), which by reason of its very vacuity is seen as profound and heartfelt.

And so it also is where romance is concerned. If one could give cogent reasons for believing that a certain person is "the one," this would itself constitute evidence to the contrary. It would suggest that one is thinking rather than feeling, and that one is expressing one's own will and desires rather than trusting in God to provide and to direct one's steps.

Which points to what is perhaps the most fundamental problem with the "you just know" approach to romantic discernment. The assumption is that thinking for yourself and trusting in God are mutually exclusive, and that God works in people's lives precisely to the degree that they allow him to do so by declining to make their own decisions. It is an appealing assumption, in the sense that it seems to offer a way to insulate oneself from the possibility of failure. If you don't make your own decisions, you can't fail. On the contrary: let God make your decisions, and you are guaranteed success.

However attractive this approach to life and love might seem, it is a mirage. No one has to "let" God work in his or her life. God is at work in people's lives all of the time, simply by virtue of the fact that God is God. The choice one has is between being more or less thoughtfully obedient to God and faithfully responsive to his grace. And there is always an element of risk involved in human decision making and in human love. You cannot know for sure how things are going to turn out. You can only do the best you can, depending on God's grace in the midst of both success and failure.

Cross-Shaped, Gospel-Centered Marriage

Martin Luther draws a contrast between what he calls a theology of glory and a theology of the cross. A theology of glory finds God in sunsets and cathedrals and anywhere else that seems magnificent and triumphant. A theology of the cross finds God in a cradle in Bethlehem, in a garden at Gethsemane, on a cross outside the walls of Jerusalem. A theology of the cross, in other words, finds God not as we might imagine or desire him to be, but as he actually is, taking upon himself the frailties and sorrows of humanity and transforming them by the mysterious power of his death and resurrection.

Too many of the judgments about marriage found in Christian romantic-advice books are, in essence, theologies of glory. While the authors of these books may say that they believe in marriage "for better or for worse," in actual practice they promise bliss, pure bliss, if only we will follow their advice about finding romance with the perfect partner who, they assure us, is part of God's plan for us. A Christian love story, a Christian wedding, a Christian marriage—all are presumed to be provinces of all the perfection that a heart formed by Hollywood could possibly desire.

But the hearts of Christians are supposed to be formed by the gospel. The gospel is a success story, but it is a paradoxical success. When Jesus, the king of glory, rides into Jerusalem, he does so on a donkey. When Jesus invites his hearers to share in his life, he does so by inviting them into his death: "If any one would come after me, let him deny himself, and take up his cross, and follow me" (Matt. 16:24 KJV). And when Jesus reconciles the world to God, he does so by himself entering into the very abyss of alienation: "My God, my God, why hast thou forsaken me?" (Matt. 27:46 KJV).

We should thus be very suspicious of any account of the Christian life or of Christian relationships that fails to have at its center these and other paradoxes characteristic of the gospel. Marriage is a good gift of God; it was, as the Book of Common Prayer reminds us, established by God in the time of man's innocency, it was sanctified by Jesus through his presence at the wedding at Cana in Galilee, and it is a symbol of the union that is betwixt Christ and the church. But marriage is not a shiningly pure showcase for all that is good and beautiful, and it is not the pinnacle of all possible loves. A person is not guaranteed bliss if he or she marries, or guaranteed woe if he or she doesn't. Marriage is part of life. It has wonderful possibilities in the economy of redemption, but then, so do other parts of life and other paths in life. And there is no path in life that does not pass through the valley of the shadow of death, in one or another of its many forms.

So if we tell our students that God does not want to write their love story, what do we tell them about how to choose a marriage partner, and how to live with that partner once chosen? At the risk of being much too concise, here is what we tell them. Choose a fellow pilgrim as a partner. In the Perfect Love Story, the wedding comes at the end. In Christian marriage, the wedding comes at the beginning—the beginning of a journey together that will take you through uncharted territory, some of which we hope will be beautiful, some of which may be challenging in the extreme, and much of which is likely to be both. For such a journey, you don't want a partner who is "perfect" (whatever that might mean). You want a partner who is competent and reliable, someone whom you would trust with your very life—because when you get married, that is exactly what you are doing.

Choose someone whose character is fertile ground for love, and strive to be such a person yourself. The Perfect Love Story assumes that you will marry only someone with whom you have "fallen in love." We have nothing against falling in love, having done so ourselves once upon a time. But being "in love" is not by itself a sufficient ground for marrying anyone, if by "in love" you mean simply that you feel ineffable palpitations when you think of the beloved. Ineffable palpitations make all manner of things more pleasant, but if they are going to get you through the hard patches of life, they had better be founded upon a solid grounding of mutual trust and respect.

Choose someone with whom you can be a part of broader communities of love and support. The Perfect Love Story is all about you. Christian marriage, if it is to endure and thrive, had better be about more than you. We live in an ever-more mobile society, one in which it is expected that we and everyone we know will move from job to job and place to place in the course of a lifetime. One reason people long for marriage in such a society is that they hope to find one person who will move with them. And one of the reasons Christian marriages falter and dissolve at the rate they do is that it is simply unreasonable to expect lone marriages to support themselves. It is like expecting lone blades of grass to hold themselves upright in a hurricane. Many of us are unaccustomed to either the demands or the rewards of the cultivation of community, but this is a fundamental Christian virtue, one that is essential to the practice of Christian marriage.

Choose to love each other in the everyday. The Perfect Love Story focuses on grand gestures (the dramatic proposal, the dream honeymoon) and big-picture aspirations (the house with the white picket fence, the 2.5 children, and the dog). Christian marriage recognizes that little things matter at least as much as big ones, and probably more so. Part of the reason many people fail to develop the kind of bond that can get them through hard times is that they forgo opportunity after opportunity to rejoice together in small blessings, and to deal intentionally and constructively with small challenges. Don't always be looking over each other's shoulder at whatever it is you want and haven't got yet. Instead, give thanks together for daily bread, share the pleasures and disappointments of the day, and in so doing root yourselves ever more firmly in the soil of a truly common life.

Finally, cherish each other today, because today is what you have. The Perfect Love Story is about living happily ever after—a curiously timeless, bloodless, future-without-end. But who knows what tomorrow may bring? What is certain is that one day there will be no more tomorrows. There is a profoundly realistic note in the Christian promise to love and to cherish "until death do us part." By "realistic," we do not mean "defeatist" or "depressing." We mean that marriage, for Christians, constitutes an opportunity to look death in the eye and choose to love anyway, because that is what God in Christ has already done on our behalf.

The Perfect Love Story has a far more powerful grip on the popular imagination—including, alas, the popular Christian imagination—than does a properly Christian theology of marriage. But as we have seen in our students, there is also a deeply felt desire for authentic, thoughtful Christian life among many young people today. By God's grace perhaps all of us, young and old alike, can come more faithfully and wholeheartedly to think and act and love in ways that are congruent with God's love for us in Christ.

GOD DOES NOT ENTERTAIN

by Jason Byassee

Why did it come about that the cinema really is often more interesting, more exciting, more human and gripping than the church? . . . The church was different once. It used to be that the questions of life and death were resolved and decided here. Why is this no longer so?

Dietrich Bonhoeffer[1]

I know what it's like to be a preacher desperate for some point of contact with an otherwise inert congregation. You can't stand the thought of another Sunday facing the same blank faces, the distracted fidgeting, and the outright snoozing. As fascinating as you think the doctrine of the Trinity is, you know it's not likely to draw "Amens." So you turn away from dusty old churchspeak toward pop culture. People love TV, movies, and music; they watch and listen to hours of it every day. Maybe if you refer to some shows or movies or songs they like, or even act a little more like Letterman, they'll be right with you. Or at least not nod off this time.

It would fit with our entertainment-obsessed age to include a bit of Hollywood on Sundays. You can hardly pump gas or check out of the grocery store without a television screen in your face now. Boredom is no longer ever mandatory. Our portable entertainment devices can be schlepped everywhere, so that if you can survive the few seconds between the runway and the air, you hardly need to interrupt your movie watching to fly. My kids have a DVD screen for the van *for each of them*. Of course, the result of this omnipresent entertainment saturation is, ironically, boredom. Bruce Springsteen once sang "57 Channels and Nothing On"; today we'd have to revise him with zeroes: 5,700 channels and nothing on. With every sort of entertainment option at our fingers at all times, we channel-surf mindlessly, hardly able to concentrate on any one choice. And if we actually have to sit in silence momentarily—say, the iPod breaks or we're stranded on the tarmac, then look out.

This is a problem for faith, to put it mildly. Great practitioners of Christian prayer insist that before we can talk to God we must get quiet. Once we get restless and bored and tired of prayer, only then are we beginning to make progress toward quiet. And if we have any hope of hearing something back from God, we must get even quieter. As one of the desert fathers, a certain Nilus, said, "The arrows of the enemy cannot touch someone who loves quiet."[2] The church gathered for worship trades on quiet as well. Not that there is no noise: we sing, read, listen to a sermon, speak out prayer requests, and so on. But the real work goes on between the words, like the unspoken vowels in the Hebrew alphabet. We speak in worship only to be spoken back to by the Word who spoke the worlds into existence and cried wordlessly at Bethlehem.

Our culture lurches in the other direction, however. So, not surprisingly, a number of gifted theologians and Christian writers have suggested we look for God eagerly in popular culture. Some run Web sites,[3] others publish books,[4] and countless more reflect on movies in preaching. Sure enough, even a cursory glance at Hollywood movies shows a deep longing, one we Christians can recognize as inchoate longing for God. Barry Taylor, an artist himself and a theological reflector on other artists, insists, "There is a very, very serious conversation going on in our culture . . . about God. And the church is not a part of it."[5] These theologians have insisted that we leap in—for when Hollywood brings up the "G" word, whether overtly (think *Da Vinci Code, The Passion of the Christ*) or covertly (*Pulp Fiction, Forrest Gump,* and anything else that explores human desire), we have something to say about it. Perhaps we can even use the inchoate longings expressed on our movie screens as a conversation starter to tell others about our faith. For we must be "ready in season and out of season," as the apostle commands—surely we can be ready to attend to the powerful demands on our desire playing out on the movie screens we turn to so often. These writers imply that "long ago God spoke to our ancestors in many and various ways by the prophets and by a Son and by preachers, but in these last days God is speaking through Hollywood" (to bowdlerize Heb. 1:1–2). Shouldn't we join them in recognizing that God is doing something entertaining?

In a word, no! God does not *entertain* humanity in Christ and his church. God does, however, *delight* us through our worship. The distinction between entertainment and delight may seem thin, but it is crucial in a way that all theology is meant to be: it keeps us from blasphemy, misspeaking about God in a way that brings harm to ourselves and others.

It's OK to Love the Movies

By the end of this essay, I am going to hammer pretty hard against the notion that movies are where God now speaks and acts. So first it seems important to make clear just how much I love movies. I love the fact that they are personal, I am moved by the way they are passionate, and I marvel at their power. Yet my own experience of film's personal, passionate, and powerful character leaves me chary of claims that through it God is actively entertaining us.

Film is personal. I can sympathize with those who speak of movies in exalted terms, because movie memories are sometimes fairly important to us. As a kid I watched the original *Star Wars* forty-eight times, without the benefit of a VCR. I still get chills when I see the fuzzy blue letters begin to roll across the black backdrop. One time, my dad kept an abusive boyfriend from physically attacking his girlfriend in a theater parking lot. It was one of my proudest moments as a kid. Of course, not everyone gets chills at *Star Wars* or remembers thrills in the cinema parking lot. My response is personal, rooted in my own character and story.

Notice what all this means: anytime we think about the movies we aren't just thinking about the movies themselves as text. We're also thinking about our personal practices of moviegoing and movie-watching, about our personal histories with movies in general or particular, and about people who make movies special to us. Like other important entertainments, movies can connect with us in very personal ways.

I recently tried to introduce my kids, aged two and four, to the joys of going to a movie. They loved it, at least at first. They got to give the ticket man their own tickets, to eat popcorn, and to gawk at the video games and the lights lining the hallway on the way into the theater. But instead of being entertained by *Ratatouille*, they were scared. After seeing the cartoon hero Remy almost shot, drowned, stabbed, poisoned, and trapped, they asked if we could leave. We were glad to oblige. They may go back when they get older or may decide to do something else with their entertainment dollars and hours. Either way, who really cares? It will be their own personal decision, and their lives will not necessarily be better or worse for it.

Not so with introducing them to the church. With church we do our best to stack the deck in favor of them falling in love with the place and spending their time, talents, and treasure there profligately, for the rest of their lives. So we took them to worship as soon as we could, sneaking out to nurse and change them. We sang them hymns to put them to sleep at night. We scheduled a baptism, flew in friends and family, put together bang-up liturgies, and dunked them into new life in Christ. We appointed godparents to help us nurture them in the faith, and stand in on Jesus's behalf for them when we parents cannot. Our attitude and action toward our sons' presence in and love of the church is profoundly different than that toward their relationship with the silver screen, because church is so much more than a personal preference among entertainment options. The church is life itself, a marriage between divinity and humanity that echoes the incarnation itself. The movies? They're entertainment, a personal lifestyle option.

Film is passionate. I remember well the overwhelming emotion I felt when I saw (this is embarrassing to admit) *Titanic*. This movie *worked*, not because of its characters—Jack seemed like a spoiled pretty boy—or because of its love affair, which seemed more the stuff of teen romance. It was the disaster movie that moved me. It was the poignancy of a great ship about to go down, that most people aboard would die, and no one knew in advance. It was Rose singing a Sunday hymn asking God to protect us "from the fury of the sea." It was Mr. Andrews, the ship's designer, lamenting to her during the sinking, "I'm sorry I couldn't build you a stronger ship, Rose." It was an Irish mother reading a story to her tiny children as they are about to drown. It was the flare fired from the ship's deck, hopelessly, into an uninterested sky. It was a priest reciting from Revelation 21 about the New Heaven and New Earth "in which there is no more pain." And then it was the final, eschatological scene, in which Jack and Rose emerge in the ship's grand stairway, applauded by all the cast and crew, taking a bow, like two actors on a stage. It felt like the resurrection of the righteous and seemed to me an inkling that even a nonreligious movie like this shows hope for heaven.

I saw *Titanic* (this is even more embarrassing to admit) eight times. I saw it repeatedly because I enjoyed the way it engaged my passion and emotion. My sense that this was a good movie, worth seeing repeatedly, grew from how it made me feel, not from what it actually said. I didn't think much about the movie until I heard a sermon from a pastor I trust. He asked, "Do we really want our teenage kids seeing this relationship put on a pedestal, in which two young people meet, supposedly fall in love, and certainly have sex *on the same day*?" With that criticism in mind, I rethought the movie (or perhaps began to really think about it for the first time): what about the elder Rose's claim, after she's told the modern-day mariners and treasure hunters about her experience on the *Titanic*, that Jack "saved her," "in every way that a person can be saved." Well, actually, no he didn't: he made her more whole in some ways, saved her from an engagement to a comically wicked suitor, and launched her on a life of free-spirited adventure. But he didn't save her in the way Christians think we most need saving. Not in the sense in which Jesus saves his people, giving us new life in the church of service and love of one another and the poor, and then in the life to come. Feelings are powerful things. But they are not always to be trusted. They can be manipulated, as any altar-calling evangelist or Hollywood exec will agree.

Film is powerful. One indication of cinema's power is that I can write about *Titanic* assuming that you can follow along far more easily than if I were writing about 2 Peter or Augustine's *City of God*. Movies become an important part of our shared stock of cultural language and images. Another indication of that power is the sheer numbers associated with movie blockbusters. *Titanic* grossed more than $600 million, making it "larger" than half the nations of the world.

Mel Gibson's *The Passion of the Christ* earned similar amounts. I was a local church pastor when *The Passion* was released. Just like thousands of other pastors out there, I arranged for a group in my little country church to go see it and discuss it afterward. It was a powerful movie, at its best a meditation on the Roman Catholic stations of the cross, and I liked it a good deal more than many liberal-leaning, academic viewers. The greatest power of this movie was not evident to me in the theater, or in our church discussion, or even when I wrote my first-ever publication on it.[6] It is the power *The Passion* continues to exert on my imagination.

It's been commented that *The Passion* is really an extended reflection on the saving mysteries of the likes that Roman Catholics do in prayer with the rosary. The Sorrowful Mysteries include contemplation of Christ's agony in Gethsemane, his being whipped and crowned, his carrying his cross, and his crucifixion. If so, this would explain Gibson's intense focus on the scourging, quite out of proportion to the event's importance in the scriptures. As a crypto-Catholic who prays the rosary, I had often contemplated those mysteries before. But every time I have since seeing the film—hundreds of times that is—I can't do so without seeing the scenes from Gibson's point of view. I can't pray now without Mel.

Our imagination is a *crucial*, almost sacred place. We can't navigate the world without it. And as such we should be careful what we feed to it. Movies feed the imagination in powerful *ways*, and because they are broadcast globally, movies create a social imagination that affects us to an enormous degree. When I think of warfare now, I cannot do so without thinking of movies. So whether it's of the *Top Gun*, military-is-cool variety, or the *Platoon* war-is-hell type, my engagement with this central human activity is inevitably filtered through film. So too with a range of crucial human endeavors: business, sexuality, gender, humor. Life imitates art and vice versa, all with very little critical attention from most of us most of the time.

So movies are often profoundly personal, passionate, and powerful. This means that they are profoundly human. They touch us, move us, sometimes motivate us to be better persons. When they do, we should thank God. For if God can work through anything—as Karl Barth once memorably put it, even through a blossoming shrub or a dead dog—then of course God can and will occasionally work through the personal connection, the passionate evocation, the powerful force of an entertainment like film. But that doesn't transubstantiate movies into a means of salvation or mean that God is the Entertainer present in, with, and under every good movie we see. In the end, movies are primarily about entertainment; a movie is still just a movie.

Sacraments, Tickets, and Icons

A joke runs around Roman Catholic circles about old Uncle Joe getting liquored up, going to the movies, and forgetting where he is, genuflecting and crossing himself before he slips into his bucket seat. His response to the silver screen is the one normally given to the reserve sacrament—no small mistake. The joke about Uncle Joe works precisely because it takes his liquor to make him bow. We laugh because we recognize that it is a mistake to claim that the risen Christ is bodily present, acting to save at the multiplex the same way he is among his gathered people.

Many writers on theology and the movies have been inclined in recent years *to speak* of the movies in sacramental terms. After all, Augustine thought there were dozens of sacraments, not Protestants' measly two, nor Roman Catholics' seemingly more abundant seven. And we've already acknowledged that God can work through film. So why not draw out further parallels between sacrament and cinema? Because the two activities have less in common than it seems at first blush. Indeed, we ought to laugh at the equation of movie and sacrament because we recognize a mistake similar to Uncle Joe's. Before engaging the specific claims of two authors who advocate a sacramental interpretation of film, let me display the problem more generally in terms of tickets and icons.

A ticket to the show. Nowadays, most churches make it very clear that you don't need any special documentation to participate in Holy Communion. It used to be otherwise in my own Methodist tradition. You used to need a ticket to come to the Lord's Table. At first glance, the older practice looks more like going to the movies, since in both cases you needed a ticket for admission. But the resemblance is only on the surface; deeper down there is a profound dissimilarity. For the "price" of receiving a ticket to the Eucharist was, in some sense, knowing that admission there is free to all and free for all. The pastor gave the tickets to persons who acknowledged that they came not as those who had earned admission, but as forgiven sinners receiving what money could never buy.

Going to the movies is another matter: tickets are now nearly $10, popcorn and a drink another $10, not to mention incidentals like transportation, parking, or a babysitter. If movies are sacramental, unlike sacraments they are certainly not free. Which makes me suspect that there is a certain bourgeois sentimentality in speaking of the movies in sacramental terms. In *Nickel and Dimed*, Barbara Ehrenreich tells of working minimum wage jobs with people who don't eat extravagantly, don't live anywhere expensive, don't get sick, don't have kids, and don't do much to entertain themselves because they can't afford it.[7] Among her many keen observations about the conversational topics of the working poor was this: her coworkers *never talked about the movies*. Now, for sure, some would see them, especially on network television, years after their release. But $10 for a ticket? That's a pretty good meal for someone who might have to choose between eating and medicine and childcare. Going to movies is a privilege of the petty bourgeoisie, mythology about ten-cent movie tickets keeping hopes alive during the Great Depression notwithstanding.

So we should be rather chary of sacramentalizing movies, or of any theology of entertainment, as God's new means of grace, precisely because it puts a price on grace and puts up a fence that keeps out the poor. But the church's life depends on the presence of those who cannot pay: the poor. "Blessed be ye poor," Jesus preaches, "for yours is the kingdom of God" (Luke 6:20 KJV).

An icon of the divine. Most churches today aren't much worried about religious art. It used to be otherwise. In fact, one of the important early disputes in the church was about whether Christians could represent God through artistic images—*icons* in Greek. In general the answer was yes, though there have been important differences between the Orthodox, Roman Catholics, and various branches of Protestantism. The Calvinist tradition, for example, has a longstanding suspicion of images. Robert Johnston suggests that this suspicion about icons is the reason people like me oppose taking movies as a sacrament. What we need, he implies, is something like Eastern Orthodoxy's great appreciation of the sacramental power of the image.

Well. Perhaps what we need first is a short lesson in church history, specifically in the conflict over images in the seventh and eighth centuries that culminated in the Second Council of Nicea in 787. The two groups that squared off in this fight are called the "iconodoules," that is, those who served icons, and the "iconoclasts" (interesting which of these two words maintains cachet in our language), who destroyed them. The Orthodox not only eventually decided that pictures of Christ, Mary, and the saints *could* be used for educational or liturgical purposes. They decided that images, icons, *must* be venerated, or else Christians would forget that God became flesh, and worship an abstraction—an idol. Before Christ's incarnation it was logical for Christians to think, with the second commandment, that God ought not be drawn in art or reverenced in worship. But with the incarnation it is now a *heresy*, strictly speaking, to deny that God's image can be drawn. And if you can draw God, you'd better venerate that image.[8]

The Orthodox have quite specific instructions for how proper icons should be written (not drawn): by a monk, with gold tempera, according to the strictures by which the various images have been painted for centuries. Three-dimensional statuary is discouraged, for it must be clear this is an image, not a copy—a window, but one through which streams not only light, but darkness. God's presence, incarnate in Christ, remains a mystery, not at all fathomed by his creatures. Icons, with their stylized images, harsh lines, "unrealistic" portrayals, are glimpses of a kingdom we cannot fathom. God is present, drawable, but superabundantly, to a degree we can't imagine.

So we should be open to God engaging us through images properly produced and properly engaged. But the conflict over icons was not finally a discovery that God is visible in all images, or even in some images despite the intentions of the artists. Rather, it was the claim that because God was visible in Christ, we may also expect to "see" God in places where God faithfully gives himself to us. Places like icons properly drawn and venerated, places like sacraments duly constituted and celebrated. And movies? Are they also places where God is drawn? Where grace is dispensed? Where those who do not venerate are not, properly speaking, Christian? Of course not. Few would agree if the question were put that way. But in unguarded moments, theological advocates of the movies come quite close.

Against the "Cinemadoules"

Pardon my coining of this barbarism. But I think it not inappropriate to the level of enthusiasm some theological writers show over the movies. Remember the iconodoules did not just say that icons were helpful for educational purposes: they argued that you *had to* reverence icons or you would forget that Jesus is God enfleshed. Writers such as Robert Johnston and Greg Garrett expand at some length on *sacramental* views of moviegoing. I don't doubt that they are right in individual instances: people get converted watching movies, they come to love Jesus more dearly, they sign up for foreign missions, and all the rest of it (they also get drunk, make love, fall asleep, and set theaters on fire, but never mind). But sacraments are not individual. And movies are not sacraments.

Johnston's prolific career of writing about the intersections between theology and culture began in a movie theater. In his recent magnum opus, *Reel Spirituality: Theology and Film in Dialogue*, he writes that watching *Becket* he "heard God calling [him] to the Christian ministry," and he followed (38).[9] And this happened not only to him: he often tells of a Catholic monk who had the same experience *in the same movie*! It must be God. "Here again is the power of film. Not only can it reveal and *redeem*, but it can also be an occasion for God to speak to the viewer" (38, my italics). He calls on Andrew Greeley for support on this score, since Greeley also writes of movies that were "sacramental" "*for him*" (249, my italics again).

It is no small thing to use the verb *redeem* in Christian parlance, any less than to use the noun *sacrament*. It is God who redeems, using sacraments, properly speaking, as both Johnston and Greeley would agree. They are using the terms in a derivative manner. Johnston is often quick to insist that many movies are simply bad, and many Christians are overly zealous to find Christ images in characters who are just that: movie characters. Some films simply have no redeeming social value and should be judged as such (clearly, he did not enjoy *Harold and Kumar Go to White Castle* as much as I did). Caveats aside, the clear thrust of his work is toward a sacramental, redemptive view of the cinema.

And this is saying too much. If something is sacramental, it should be treasured in the church as a means of grace. We should direct others there. For God has promised to meet us there. It is not inappropriate to bow in the presence of a sacrament. To eat it. To bathe in it. To be anointed by it. To count on God to bring about salvation, body and soul, in this life and the next. Furthermore, sacraments are not individual activities. The power of Johnston's vignette about the stranger having the same experience as he in the same movie is its faux catholicity. A bridge has been built across time and space from one man to another, who are now, wonder of wonders, brothers. This is precisely the power of Christian sacraments. Every time we take the Eucharist God links us with everyone else who celebrates the Eucharist throughout time and space.

Johnston, a professor at Fuller Theological Seminary, is too good a theologian not to defend his cinemadoulism theologically. His prescription is for a "theology from below" (91). That is, he does not want to let Christians hide God in abstractions; he wants them to seek for God in the messiness of our daily lives. After all, God has "blessed all of creation, including human culture," according to Genesis (93). God's command to us to have dominion over the earth means, "All that we do, we do in the power of the God who created us. This includes the making of images," that is, films (105). It is no surprise that Johnston draws so deeply from Israel's Wisdom literature, both in a previous book on Ecclesiastes, and here especially on the Book of Proverbs.

My fear is that Johnston has leaned too far toward the universal in his telling of the scriptural story, and forgotten the particular; that is, that a specific God chose a particular people, Israel, to be his people in the world. To be, as Michael Wyschogrod has put it, a corporate incarnation: God embodied. God's electing, embodying way is not negated but fulfilled in Jesus, and in the church that is the limbs to Jesus's body.[10] A slip of Johnston's pen may be more revealing than he intends. Writing of the way in which Israel was often schooled in God's ways, ironically enough, by Gentiles, he writes (in parenthesis): "the Israelites (who believed they were

'God's people') were threatened by the Assyrians (who certainly were not 'God's people')" (100). Wait—the Israelites believed this because *they were* God's people, and indeed *still are* (Rom. 11:26). The Assyrians, like the rest of us Gentiles, certainly were not and are not God's people unless we are engrafted there by Christ.

Johnston's preference for the universal over the particular is echoed in Greg Garrett's recent book *The Gospel according to Hollywood*.[11] Garrett is a highly successful novelist and short-story writer, just beginning a promising career as a theologian. Garrett writes beautifully, and even more daringly, in favor of the analogies between film and worship. As a moviegoer of the new generation, Garrett was moved by *Pulp Fiction* the way Johnston was by *Becket*. As a skilled writer, he appeals to a more literary source for justification: Gerard Manley Hopkins's great line, "The world is charged with the grandeur of God" (xviii). The incarnation means we should seek God "in our creations" as well as in God's. This is a particularly Anglican theological move: to speak of the incarnation as God's sanctification of all that is. Or, to use Stanley Hauerwas's description, in the incarnation God comes down, looks around, and says, "Looks pretty good to me!" There is no crucifying, raising, and transforming work to be done in creation on this account.[12]

Garrett is not content to look for abstract epiphanies. He's willing to see trinitarian relations in the act of film projection itself. God is timeless, unintelligible, just like the reel of film over there in the corner— until light shines through it, and it comes to life. "This is how Christians think of the man called Jesus . . . through the linear life of Jesus we can begin to understand the story of God in human terms" (27). The analogy fails because it suggests a kind of modalism—a heresy the early church rejected: God is really one, showing up in three different guises. The Trinity teaches that God is not only three in his appearances among us, but three also in his eternal life; indeed, that the incarnation is God's eternal tripartite love "turned outward" toward creation. There is no eternal relationship of mutual adoration between the reel and its projection on screen. The relationship between film reel and projected intelligibility somehow falls short of this mystery.

As does another image: that of the three lead characters in *The Matrix*, Neo, Trinity, and Morpheus (28). They are "three individuals who operate as a team, a unit." But that would suggest that God is three people, not three persons. Three people do not determine one another's identity, even three as close as those three—Trinity and Neo's sexual relationship, Morpheus's mentorship of them both, and so on. Any one of them can be killed and the others can live on. Garrett's boldness is to be commended: if you seek God in the movies, you should be convinced you can find him there! So Christ images abound in *Cool Hand Luke*, *Spiderman 2*, and *E.T.* Garrett is clear these are analogies, and like any analogy they equivocate at points. All the same, I'm dubious whether those are analogies that get at the mystery of the God whom Christians worship: the blessed Trinity, one of whom became incarnate and rose for our salvation.

Johnston's and Garrett's conclusions are spot-on: Christians should be learning from and in dialogue with the movies. Why? Well, by my lights, because we're middle-class Americans, and middle-class Americans go to movies. There is indeed a vibrant conversation about God going on in secular culture, above all in films. Christians are participant in that conversation insofar as we go to and argue about movies. The flap over *The Da Vinci Code* was just a remarkably widespread outgrowth of this conversation. It is appropriate, then, for ministers to conduct study groups on films, to hold sessions of "popcorn theology," and to use films with the youth group, as our authors suggest. Maybe even—and I say this very hesitantly—to use clips of films in worship. But a great caveat must be raised. The visual word is powerful. If a clip is used in worship, folks are likely to remember how cool worship was: "The pastor showed us a movie!"[13] But they are unlikely to enter more deeply into the worship of God. Films are not bad. I'm not for launching a new English Reformation that would go around smashing images. But if we speak of them in sacramental terms, as sites of worship, then *cinemaclasm* would not be inappropriate.

What Movies Are For

One thing we can expect of the movies is for them to take us by surprise. Both Garrett and Johnston justly praise Paul Thomas Anderson's *Magnolia*. At a climactic point in the film, a plague of frogs falls from the sky: a clear echo of the exodus. This sort of bizarre, unimaginable, otherworldly intervention could only come from a film. And a film that didn't tip its hand at that: the dinosaurs in *Jurassic Park* aren't surprising; they're on the marquee. But the frogs in *Magnolia* are totally unexpected. They suggest a God beyond our analogies, beyond our plotting, and yet are an echo of an ancient scriptural story that might—who knows?—erupt anew in our day.

Many films echo the Christian tradition by no accident: they are firmly rooted within it. This is of course the case with the film adaptations of J. R. R. Tolkien's *Lord of the Rings* trilogy. Neither of our two cinemadoule authors makes much of Peter Jackson's films, perhaps because it's too easy to hear the God of Jesus reflected in Gandalf's rebuke of Frodo: "Don't be so quick to mete out death and judgment," or even in the movie slogan: "All that is gold does not glitter." The ring itself echoes the Roman Catholic moral tradition that insists one cannot use unjust means (the ring) for just ends (bringing peace), though every character is tempted to do precisely that.

My own favorite echo of the Christian tradition is more unintentional, and perhaps more reflective of the pagan Norse imagery Tolkien also loved than of the Bible. When the fellowship is threatened by the Bal-Rog and Gandalf throws himself into the breach to save it, he throws out an incantation of some sort. "I am the keeper of the sacred fire, wielder of the flame of Anor. You shall not pass!" Keeper of what? From where? It doesn't matter. The bridge gives way, the monster is gone, though taking Gandalf with him (in an echo of Christ's descent into hell). The efficacy of the incantation depends in no way on its intelligibility. These words work because, well, they're magic, and Gandalf is powerful, and good wins—despite evil's cunning. Even to explain it like that is to let its power diminish, like letting the air leak from a tire. But it's true on film somehow.

A final example: the climax of *Fight Club*, a film justly praised by our interlocutors. In the film's final scene the "VISA building" and others of the world's temples of consumer credit crash to the ground in act of terror perpetrated by the fight club. This could not really happen, of course. Credit is too omnipresent around the globe; there is no single skyline that could be decimated to take all our credit histories with it. And that's precisely the point: what can't happen in real life *can* happen in film. It's a violent instantiation of the year of Jubilee: debts forgiven, slaves set free. "If you're not a pacifist, that's what you should be doing," a friend of mine says, emitting just a bit of Christian anarchism.

Movies are good at showing the counterintuitive on a large scale. Theater can't quite do this—Broadway goers' gawking over the helicopter in *Miss Saigon* proves the point. Paint and sculpture cannot quite either: surrealism can portray, say, a melting clock, but images of miracles don't quite evoke the awe. A film can portray the world more or less like it is. And then *bam!* God intervenes. Usually with humor. Always to save.

But these are just glimmers, glimpses, spy-holes of grace. Not the flooding torrent of grace that is God's promised presence in his sacraments. They are catch-as-catch-can. Not even all the people seeing the same movie at the same time will see them. But some will. Rejoice! Talk about it in Sunday school. It's a worthy topic. And even when it doesn't strike your religious fancy, a movie can be a staggering success. Remember the first time you saw "bullet time" in *The Matrix*. When Trinity leaps up, freezes, and the camera rotates before she kicks that agent, you went, "Whoa, that's freaking awesome!" Didn't you? It's still awesome even without a theological gloss.

But it's not a sacrament. You can't eat it. You oughtn't reverence it. It doesn't make all its partakers one body or turn them into Christ's body for the restoration of creation. Movies are light, image, story, song—in short, great entertainment. But they are not God's chosen means to save.

Divine Delight

At a key point in *Confessions*, Augustine marvels at the way we love a good story. "God of goodness, what causes man to be more delighted by the salvation of a soul who is despaired of but is then liberated from great danger than if there has always been hope or if the danger has only been minor?"[14] Like most of the good questions in *Confessions*, Augustine has no full answer to this one. For whatever reason, the father's joy is greater when the prodigal returns than if he had never left. "Tears flow at the joy of the solemnities of your house when in your house the story is read of your younger son, 'who was dead and is alive again, was lost and has been found' (Luke 15:32)." God seems simply to have arranged the universe such that we love a good story, with a crisis in the middle, and an unexpected, but happy, ending.

In one way, Augustine's *Confessions* is a retelling of the prodigal-son story: he who grew up with a devout mother, drinking in Jesus's name with her milk. Then he wandered far from his loving Creator, wallowing in the filth of ambition, lust, and pride. But miracle of miracles, he came to his senses and returned to God's house. And not by his own devices, but because God fleshed himself in the story of which he is Author, "and emptied himself . . . to the point of death" (Phil. 2:7–8 NRSV). It's the story at the heart of things, participated in and re-presented anew by all who dwell in God's house. Augustine's great work is an effort to show the reorientation of his desire away from himself, and his lust for money, satisfaction, and power, and toward the God who alone can truly satisfy. The church has been trying to do the same ever since.

At their best, movies, like all good stories, show glimpses of this Story at the heart of things. We shouldn't be surprised that filmmakers would occasionally, perhaps unwittingly, tell our story far better than we do. Especially in a post-Christian culture with residually religious ideas still "in the water": an afterlife for those who do good, a presumption against intolerance, an obligation to help those in need, and so on (these ideas are more like G. K. Chesterton's antidote against genuine Christianity than the real thing, but never mind). Christian theologians attending the movies see much of our best "stuff" there, because the movies are also after human desire at the most basic level. And sometimes they touch our most cherished desires better than worship does.

Christians have long struggled to account for the presence of truth in communities far removed from the church. Origen of Alexandria came up with a metaphor that had a great deal of staying power on this score: Christians borrowing from Plato is akin to the Israelites plundering the Egyptians. In the Exodus the fleeing Israelites took all of Pharaoh's valuables. How was this not theft? Well, they took it to beautify the temple they would build one day. And further, the valuables were not his at all, but God's. So it is with philosophy: what Plato says that is true is not really from him, but from the source of all Truth. On a less metaphorical level, some Christians speculated that Plato bumped into Jeremiah at some point, and the prophet taught him the best of what he knew. Augustine backtracked on this when someone showed him the chronology was all wrong, but he still held out a suspicion that somehow Plato got his hands on scripture. How else could he have taught so much truth?

Medieval Christians had to make sense of how their Jewish and Muslim philosophical interlocutors knew so much, even if that knowledge did not add up to salvation in the Christians' eyes. They turned to less conspiratorial accounts than Augustine was given to: surely a good Creator will have given his good creatures a great deal of access to the truth. Thomas Aquinas even wished to dial down the enthusiasm for "natural law," insisting it could not grant saving knowledge of God. All the same our creation in the image of God means that fallen, sinful creatures can actually have a great deal of purchase on truth. On this view it's no surprise that even quite non-Christian filmmakers would get so much right.[15]

The Reformers tended to heap opprobrium on what they took as the medievals' optimism about the amount of truth one could know without relationship to the Truth in Christ. Karl Barth, the twentieth century's greatest theologian, worried that such a view of natural knowledge of God so opened the door to abuse that its result could be the German Christians—those who felt Adolf Hitler and the German people are the fulfillment of God's desire for humanity. He rebuked all natural knowledge of God with a sharp "Nein!" Yet he himself later had to account for how those far outside the church could get so much *right,* even far more right than the church many times. His solution: secular parables. Those far from grace can live and think in ways that call the church to account, teach us what we did not know, and draw us to convert anew to the lordship of Christ. This is no natural optimism about our ability to reason, far from it. It's a view of Jesus's lordship as so exalted that there is nowhere that it does not shine. Not even in Hollywood (though Barth doesn't say that!).[16]

I offer these approaches to truth outside the church to show that theologians have long wrestled with the problem pointed to by Johnston and Garrett. But they have done so with a good deal more circumspection. It is actually a puzzle for most of church history how the unredeemed could show redemption so much more clearly than the redeemed, at times. But notice what happens if we simply say God is speaking through the unredeemed, full stop. The puzzle disappears. Or better yet, the mystery vanishes. "God is speaking through the movies! The movies are sacraments!" is a clarion call to make God's appearance in unexpected places into something commonplace. We should let the difficulty remain: how is it exactly that God speaks through pagan philosophy? Other religions? The multiplex? How surprising. Who knew?[17]

And we should not forget how close our reaction to the movies is to the reaction we ought to have in worship. It is Christian worship that is meant to draw our desire for God back to its rightful place. It is in the church we learn anew to love God first, and to love all other people (especially the poor, our enemies, those we don't like) on the way to eternal life with God. So the church and the theater compete, at least partially, on the same playing field. The church cannot afford to let the theater have a monopoly on desire (note: the church knows this, or it wouldn't be using movie clips!).[18]

A certain Quodvultdeus of Carthage, a fourth-century bishop and teacher, saw this clearly.[19] Like all early Christian preachers, he admonished his people to flee from the circus, the coliseum, the theater: animals eating slaves and nude jesters entertaining drunk spectators was not any sort of thing Christians should be part of: "Beloved, flee the spectacles, flee the devil's most wicked theater seats, lest the chains of the evil one bind you." But he was not simply priggish about his prohibitions: "But if your soul must be entertained, and it delights in being a spectator, Holy Mother Church displays wholesome spectacles for veneration which may entertain your minds by their attraction and not destroy but guard the faith in you." The problem is not just that people are naked or eaten in secular entertainment. It is that the desire touched upon and thrilled by such entertainment is precisely the desire God means to use to draw his people back to himself.

The entire pleasure of it is this: to cheer, because one whom the devil conquers now conquers others; to leap up and down and jeer, because the enemy's side has lost his horse. . . . Contrast our holy, healthy, and most agreeable spectacles. Consider in the book of the Acts of the Apostles the man crippled from his mother's womb; although he had never walked, Peter made him run. . . . think about what you ought to look at and consider where you ought to cheer: there where sound horses are crippled or here where crippled people are healed? (25)

Remember how Augustine spoke of the tears in church when the story of the prodigal son is read (Bible reading is apparently a bigger thrill when you don't have cable!). The heart that leaps in the circus, in the multiplex, is meant actually to leap at God's work in Christ, at making the lame to walk and the blind to see. And the movies, like the ancient circus, can actually be a hindrance to that.

It is no accident that the movies have shown themselves expert of late at depicting a Gnostic worldview—that is, a view of "salvation" that shows this world is not the real one, there is actually a hidden, *more* real world "behind" it, that can be discovered by those genuinely in the know. Everyone walking around thinks these bodies are our real selves, but they're saps—true knowledge, *gnosis*, involves an escape from this faux world. In *The Truman Show*, Jim Carrey's character finally realizes Christof (hint, hint) is a sham, and real life is outside the bubble. In *The Matrix*, the machines' fake world is shown for what it is: a means to imprison humans so our bodies can be used for energy. The good guys make occasional raids back into the computer matrix to save others of us, but it's no place to live the good life. And, of course, *The Da Vinci Code* quite openly professes its preference for ancient Christian Gnostics over orthodox believers (though why anyone would think the Gnostics are to be preferred on matters of sex, gender, and the body is beyond me. Literally).

The movies are perfect as a Gnostic medium because they beam ideas to our mind. Our bodies are occupied, hopefully by comfortable bucket seats, fresh popcorn, and maybe a hand held in another's. But that's just to keep us comfortable for two hours of brain work. I've seen plenty of people give their lives for others on screen—Jesus a dozen or so times, plenty of soldiers, gobs of parents and friends. But I've never seen someone in a movie theater give their life for an actual, flesh-and-blood human being. Augustine, after he has become a priest, marvels at the fleshy nature of his good work: "I think upon the price of my redemption, and I eat it and drink it, and distribute it. In my poverty I desire to be satisfied from it together with those who 'eat and are satisfied' (Ps. 61:5). 'And they shall praise the Lord who seek him' (Ps. 21:27)." Movies are amazing, marvels, even miracles. But God's church, where God meets us in judgment and grace: that's really where the action is.[20]

Ancient Christian thinkers thought we only *have* desire at all as a God-given means by which we can be borne aloft toward God. This is why they saw in biblical texts like the Song of Songs an icon of divine and human love. This depiction of the height of human love—sexual intimacy—could not but be an image of divine love for humanity. Anything that engages human desire and attempts to meet it is on holy ground, however unaware much of the time. We Christians are graced to know that the height of intimacy between divine love and human receptivity is the incarnation of Christ, extended by the Spirit into the life of the church. Wherever we see delight engaged, we see glimpses of what God is doing with us. Occasionally we cheer, occasionally we boo, and always we ought to take notice. But it is only a glimpse. In Christ we have a vision of God that is unending, everlasting, glory itself.

6

GOD DOES FATHER, SON, AND HOLY SPIRIT

D. Brent Laytham

The title of this chapter does not contain a typo; the word *does* is not a misprint for *is*. The fact that a reader might assume the editor has gotten sloppy here is evidence of the fact that *is* is the verb of choice for statements about the triune identity of God. And of course God *is* Father, Son, and Holy Spirit, a truth revealed in scripture and affirmed in the church's historic creeds. But *God also does who God is*, as it will be the burden of this chapter to show.

Let me begin with a story that illustrates the need for reflection on this topic. A few years ago at the seminary where I teach, one of our best theology students preached an excellent sermon in chapel. I was particularly pleased, for I not only teach theology but am also convinced that theologically rich sermons are as crucial for the church as they are rare. So I was feeling all warm and fuzzy at the service's end, when our student pronounced the benediction in the name of the "Creator, Redeemer, and Sustainer." It was a bucket of cold water poured all over my theological contentment, a kick in the stomach of my professorial pride.

Why was I so startled and disappointed by a way of naming God that has become common in American churches? Because it badly distorts three pressing theological issues: God's action, God's name, and God's relation to the world. The phrase "Creator, Redeemer, and Sustainer" misstates what God is doing in the world, misunderstands the meaning of the revealed name "Father, Son, and Holy Spirit," and obscures the character of God's relation to the world.

Now don't get me wrong. I'm not telling this story to reprimand a student after all these years. If anything, I commend her for recognizing that all three of these issues are crucial for theology and central to discipleship. The church needs more pastors who are willing to grapple with the hard tasks of careful description of God's ongoing work, of exquisite care with God's holy name, of clear articulation of God's relation to us. But it is also important that we settle for nothing less than the full articulation of what God has done for us and shown to us in Jesus Christ.

So I will turn to each of these three issues—God's action, name, and relation—to sketch out why "Creator, Redeemer, and Sustainer" falls short. This will move us toward a richer understanding of the Trinity, one that allows us to see and say that what God does is who God is.

Divine Doing

What does God do in, with, and for the world? The "Creator, Redeemer, Sustainer" formula suggests that there are three things God does: God makes the world in the first place, God fixes it when things go wrong, and then . . . what? God sustains, as in holds things in continued existence? Well, in one sense I hope so. I hope my house is still there when I go home tonight, that

Duke will still have a basketball team next year, that not even the gates of hell should prevail against Christ's church, not to mention hoping that my wife and children continue to exist. But there are a whole host of things I hope are not sustained a second longer: child abuse, racism, cancer, reality television shows, hunger, thirst, violence, and, most of all, sin.

The problem with *sustain* as a fundamental way of naming God's relation to the world is that it doesn't go anywhere. It both misunderstands the doctrine of creation and fails to follow the narrative arc of the biblical story. Of course, it does get right the truth that God continues to hold in existence all that is, that moment by moment nothing would be at all if God did not sustain its existence (Ps. 104:30–31). But Christian theology has not traditionally thought that this sustaining was a separate action from creation itself. This is where the analogy between God's making and our making breaks down. For us, making is one thing, sustaining another. Chevrolet's workforce made my car in the first place, but I (and my mechanic, Zuhar) must sustain it over time by our care. With God, on the other hand, the original making and the ongoing sustaining are all part of the one complex action we call creation. Technically, theology has called this the doctrine of creation out of nothing, *creatio ex nihilo*. Most simply it means that God both originally and continually is the one and only reason for all that is. Creation is what God *lets be* in the first place and *keeps being* continually.[1] This is the doctrinal claim that "Sustainer" fractures.

Worse, however, is the way "Sustainer" seems to cut us off from the hoped-for conclusion of the biblical narrative. The scriptural story is a pilgrimage from good beginning to better end; it narrates a romance between God and the world that finally ends in perfected love, joy, and peace. Thus, we live not with an expectation that things will merely be sustained, but rather with a hope that they will finally be completed by the "pioneer and perfecter of our faith" (Heb. 12:2 NRSV).

Theology has traveled two different paths to emphasize that creation's story will be brought by God to a glorious completion. One has been eschatology—theological reflection on the resurrection victory and coming again of Jesus Christ. From the perspective of eschatology, "Creator, Redeemer, Sustainer" implies that we've given up on Christ's returning to consummate the kingdom and to make all things whole. The other path by which theology has emphasized the future glory intended for all of creation is pneumatology—theological reflection on the Holy Spirit. Most simply, the focus of the Spirit's activity is not to maintain things as they are now, but to perfect them as God intends for them finally to be. From the perspective of pneumatology, "Creator, Redeemer, Sustainer" implies that we've forgotten the primary working of the Spirit to perfect and, under the conditions of sin, to renew creation.[2]

Now at this point someone might think that we could fix the whole problem by changing to "Creator, Redeemer, Perfecter." But that won't work either, because the three persons of the Trinity do not act separately, as if one does the work of creating, another does the work of redeeming, and finally the Holy Spirit comes along to finish the job. God's doing is far more integral than that, as we shall see below. Suffice it to say here that whenever God does something, all three persons of the Trinity are doing it together precisely because God is these three persons doing what they do. God is not a team that takes turns, not a troupe that plays parts, and certainly not a committee of persons who act independently of one another.[3] Rather, the one God is Father, Son, and Holy Spirit together doing all that God does.[4]

Moreover, speaking of the Triune God by way of three activities miscounts what God does. On the one hand, God does infinitely more than three things. How could we ever limit what God does to just three activities? The scriptures are replete with God's doings: God asks and answers; God blesses and bears; God creates, calls, and cleanses, God speaks and seeks and saves. Given all this doing, any list of actions short enough to count on one hand will necessarily involve grouping divine action into larger categories. For example, God's calling, delivering, forgiving, guiding, and healing can all be included within the broader category of redemption. Such summarizing can be helpful theological work.

Which brings us to the other hand: we can and should characterize all that God does under two summary actions rather than three—creation and redemption. Most basically, what God does in relation to all that is not God can be reduced to these two activities: making it to be and setting it right; giving and forgiving;[5] creating and saving. All God's doing, from "in the beginning" to kingdom come, is the two activities of creating and redeeming.[6]

To summarize our investigation so far: I've argued that our one God who is three persons does two distinct things, and that both doings are the work of all three. Given this, a more fitting benediction might be "now the blessing of God the Father, Son, and Holy Spirit, our Creator and Redeemer, be upon you all." Such would more properly name the Triune God and more accurately number God's works.

Divine Naming

The point of novel formulations like "Creator, Redeemer, Sustainer" is to disavow a perceived patriarchy in the traditional nomenclature of Father and Son. This point cannot be casually dismissed. As Catherine Mowry LaCugna notes, "There is no doubt that the use of only masculine images and metaphors in worship and in theology creates the impression that God is male."[7] And that impression, coupled with two millennia of sexism and patriarchy, has been profoundly detrimental to the full flourishing of women. So any discussion of how we name the three persons who are God must begin with the categorical denial that God is male or masculine.

The attraction of "Creator, Redeemer, Sustainer" is precisely that it avoids gender. Creating, after all, is done by both women and men, so the name "Creator" implies nothing abut God's sex. Redeeming is also an equal opportunity activity, so "Redeemer" bypasses the gender worry. It fittingly titles Jesus of Nazareth but also names quite fittingly what Ruth was for Naomi and what Esther became for her people. Likewise, "Sustainer" is a gender-free role, though studies of American households continue to find that most of the sustaining work done there is done by women.

This suggests one problem with naming the Triune persons by functional roles. We are tempted to cozy up with divinity. Some theologians now urge us to think of ourselves as "co-creators" with God. Others even style some of our heroes (Gandhi, King, etc.) as "co-redeemers" with Christ.[8] Such a blurring of the difference between God and us is not the inevitable result of the Creator-Redeemer-Sustainer strategy, and I don't mean to damn it by referring to such an obvious excess.

Yet even where a proper distinction is maintained between divine doing and (responsive) human doing,[9] there is still good reason for Christians to prefer the scriptural and creedal language of Father and Son; namely, these are the designations used of and by Jesus at revelatory moments in his interaction with God. In the waters of baptism and on the mount of transfiguration, God says "this is my Son." Teaching on the mountain, comforting in the upper room, struggling in the garden, and dying on the cross, Jesus addresses God as Father. No wonder, then, that Paul describes our redemption itself as participating in this mode of speaking: "And because you are children, God has sent the Spirit of his Son into our hearts, crying, 'Abba! Father!'" (Gal. 4:6 NRSV). And no wonder that Jesus teaches us to address God by praying "Our Father. . . ."

The Triune names "father" and "son" indicate relations that are active and ongoing. "Father" is not first about how God relates to the world in general, but to the Son in particular. It ought to bring to mind the claim of unique relation in John 3:16, that this Son is God's "only begotten." As the theological tradition reflected on John's claim, it came to see that such a begetting could not have a beginning in time, lest there be a time before the Son was begotten, a time before there was a Son. If such were the case, it would mean either that the Father is the real Deity, and the Son at best a godlike creature, or that there is an unknown God behind the one we know as Father and Son (and Holy Spirit, though this didn't figure much in the original debate). Instead, theological reflection on the event of Jesus Christ led the church to the claim that the Son is "eternally begotten of the Father."

All of this means, therefore, that using "Father" as a divine name should not send us looking for ways that God fathers the world. To call God "Father" is not to suggest that fathering is somehow the basic divine action—what God does in, with, and for the world. Which brings us the long way round to a final reason to be done with the Creator-Redeemer-Sustainer formula: the divine doing implicit in the name Father, Son, and Holy Spirit is prior to, and indeed the source of, God's creating and redeeming work. To put it more simply, "Father" is not first a claim about how God loves the world, but rather about how the first divine person loves the second.[10] Only because of that love does the Triune God create the world and then redeem it. If "Father" intended primarily to articulate how God relates to the world, then it would become applicable to God only when God creates everything else. Whatever God was before that would be hidden and unknowable.

Divine Relating

I have one last concern with Creator-Redeemer-Sustainer: it skews our understanding of God's relation to the world. This claim is not self-evident, since naming God by active role invites us to ask about the relation of agent and object.[11] "Creator?" raises the question "Creator of what?" "Redeemer" invites the question

"Redeemer of whom?" So calling God "Creator-Redeemer-Sustainer" seems to help us focus on the God–world relationship. And since I've just argued that "Father" and "Son" fundamentally express the relation of the first two Triune persons, rather than the relation of God to the world, when it comes to divine relating the newer trinitarian formula might seem superior to the traditional one.[12]

Yet it is not superior, because it gets God's relation to the world wrong in two ways. First, it is impersonal language, whereas the deity we encounter in the scriptural story is profoundly personal.[13] Granted, in our experience, the activities of creating and redeeming are largely done by persons, so we wouldn't typically expect "Creator" or "Redeemer" to reference a robot, rooster, or rock. But we also know from experience that we are more than what we do, which means that the fullness of who we are—our personhood—is not conveyed even by such central nominalizations as teacher or pastor or friend. The problem here is not that we've all had many different teachers, pastors, and (I hope) friends, as if to call God "creator" were to leave open the question, Which one? Theologically, creating and redeeming are singular activities of a single agent—God. So "Creator" and "Redeemer" implies just one agent who does the creating and redeeming work. But given the way language must stretch analogically when used of God, these terms finally neither say that God is personal nor show us what shape the personal takes in God.

Let me illustrate with two historical examples of belief systems in which a deity that is "creator" either is not personal or is personal in a manner entirely other than that of the God of Jesus Christ. On the one hand, Aristotle's philosophy demonstrates the way one can believe in a Creator that is entirely impersonal. What shapes the world as we know it, according to Aristotle, is the attractive power of the unmoved mover, a divinity that has no active, intentional relation with anything outside itself, let alone some form of personal interaction with creatures. On the other hand, Marcion's mongrelization of Christianity demonstrates the way one can believe in a personal Creator who is entirely different from the one we encounter in the biblical canon.[14] Who made the world, according to Marcion, is a minor deity too stupid to make a really good world and too mean to care. Thus both Aristotle and Marcion espouse a Creator of sorts, but Aristotle's is decidedly not personal, and Marcion's is personal but repugnant. Neither one is the personal God of biblical, Christian faith.

Even when we do intend to refer to the decisively personal and infinitely loving God revealed in Jesus Christ, we fail to adequately convey this with Creator-Redeemer-Sustainer language. Because this formula reads like a job description, and because it refers to God by God's accomplishments, it leaves a gap—either potential or real—between what God does and who God is. It raises the possibility of a "God behind God," a deity who creates and redeems (and whatever else), but who doesn't fully "show up" in the process. To the contrary, Christian faith asserts that God really does show up, that God really is *personally present* in divine doing. As Paul says, "in Christ God was reconciling the world" (2 Cor. 5:19 NRSV). And as Catherine of Siena prays, "What more could you have given me than the gift of your very self?"[15]

So if the first weakness of "Creator, Redeemer, Sustainer" is its inability to convey the truth that God's relation to the world is linked fundamentally to who God is, its second flaw is the failure to notice that *who God is shapes God's doing*. Put most simply, the Triune God does all things trinitarianly. Divine doing is not parceled out among the persons of the trinity; we couldn't sneak up on the Holy Spirit comforting Christians while the Father and Son sit idly by. And the same is true for the redemption that Jesus brings; it is the will and work of the Father, empowered and made real to us by the Holy Spirit (see Gal. 4:4–6). If we consider God's creating work, the point becomes even clearer: where theologians have thought that creation is uniquely what God the Father does, the result is almost inevitably a doctrine that the Son and Spirit are finally creatures, even if unique and especially powerful ones.[16]

So there's no danger that any one of the trinitarian persons will break up the band to launch a solo tour. All three triune persons are working in everything God does. But their common work does not make it impossible to tell the three persons apart. The biblical story shows us that God's action has a consistently trinitarian shape; for example, to save the world the Father sends the Son in the power of the Spirit. Every divine action involves the Father initiating what the Son mediates and the Spirit perfects. Creator-Redeemer-Sustainer doesn't just fail to show us that; it actively obscures our seeing it.

It is time to move to the positive phase of my argument. But as we do so, it is important to note the progress we've already made in understanding the claim that God does who God is. In the section on divine action, we saw that the one God who is three persons does two things—create and redeem. Turning to divine naming, we saw that naming the three persons of the Trinity speaks first and more fundamentally about their active relation with one another, rather than about what they do in and for creation. Finally, my consideration of divine relating showed us that who God is shapes God's doing in and for the world.

God Does

In his *Theology of the Old Testament*, Walter Brueggemann eloquently notes that "the characteristic claim of Israel's testimony is that Yahweh is an active agent who is the subject of an active verb."[17] These active verbs are usually quite powerful, depicting "an action that is transformative, intrusive, or inverting" (123). Brueggemann notes five things that God characteristically does: God creates, makes promises, delivers, commands, and leads (145–204). Though not typically the only actor, God is characteristically "the primary actor" (205), the incomparable "alterative Agent" (209) whose action invites response.

Likewise, we find in the New Testament the same typical grammar—God as the subject of strong, active verbs—and the same characteristic testimony—divine action invites and enables transformative response. Yet this witness now shines through a christological lens. "Long ago God *spoke* . . . by the prophets, but in these last days he *has spoken* to us by a Son, whom he *appointed* heir of all things, through whom he also *created* the worlds" (Heb. 1:1–2 NRSV); "in Christ God *was reconciling* the world to himself" (2 Cor. 5:19 NRSV); "For God so *loved* the world that he *gave* his only Son" (John 3:16 NRSV); "This Jesus God *raised* up" (Acts 2:32 NRSV). Moreover, this Christ-focused testimony to divine doing is enabled and empowered by the Holy Spirit.[18]

Thus, our two-testament canon bears witness to an active God who is Father, Son, and Holy Spirit. All of scripture depicts the doings of God. Moreover, scripture says that its own testimony is a product of divine action, that we know God's acts only because God acts to help us know them. In other words, we are able to know what God does because God helps us to know. Of course, even with God's help there are limits to our understanding. This is because what God does is unlike any human doing. Even though we describe divine doing using verbs drawn largely from the human domain—*speak, give, love, promise,* and so on—when these verbs have the living God as their subject, the noun, as it were, commandeers the verb. Language gets stretched beyond our ability to control its meaning or even fully to understand it. Thus, when God is the subject of the sentence, we should say that our verbs are being used analogously rather than literally. They help us say something true about what God does even though we can never fully understand it.

This leads to a second limit on our understanding of what God does. Even if we accept that verbs assigned to serve the divine Subject have been commandeered for tasks too grand, we might still want to press for a logical and coherent account of how it is possible for God to act in or on creation. Acknowledging that the words *create, promise, command, lead, redeem,* and *speak* are at best analogically applicable to what God does, we might still feel compelled to ask, "How does God do that?"—a question very similar to the one Mary posed to Gabriel at the annunciation: "How can this be?" (Luke 1:34 NRSV). Gabriel's answer, implicitly Trinitarian, is that God will do this wonderful thing. That will hardly satisfy the demands of a modern, rationalistic mind convinced that "the causal nexus in space and time" leaves no place or possibility for God to act.[19] But perhaps it can shed light on how we should approach the question of accounting for divine activity in, on, and for our world. Though Gabriel uses a lot of words, he most fundamentally answers the "how?" question by saying that God is God, thereby refocusing Mary's attention from a "how" she could never understand to a "who" that she can fundamentally trust. Note how this same question can be raised even more fundamentally of the very core of the gospel: "the God of Israel has raised his servant Jesus from the dead."[20] Obviously, one could respond to this proclamation with the question "How did God do that?" But we don't have to wait for a successful answer to the "how?" question in order to determine whether this is good news or not. Indeed, here as elsewhere, "we can attribute actions to God without claiming to understand how God performs those actions."[21] Christianity is not an explanation of *how* God can act in the world; it is a proclamation *that* God has acted to redeem the world. It is a gospel, not a theory.

God Does Triunely

Too much talk about what God does or doesn't do in the world bypasses the Son and the Spirit, either by claiming an immediacy that does violence to the mode of divine working in our world, or by claiming an intentionality that violates the shape of God's action in the Spirit and the Son. In the first error, people will say that "God did" something, yet ignore two or even all three of the Triune persons. Apparently, the "god" they mean is not triune, or is triune but does some things one divine person at a time. In the second error, people will interpret some event as divine doing without considering God's self-revelation in Jesus and the Spirit. This error fails to discern the triune character of divine action. Both of these errors are avoidable by a Trinitarian theology that begins with, and refuses to leave behind, the simple truth that in Jesus, God goes on a mission.

First, the triune pattern of divine action. Early Christians recognized that in Jesus "they had, in some sense, encountered God firsthand."[22] Not an angel, not an emissary, not a prophet, not a messenger, not any kind of intermediary who, though not God, nonetheless represents God. Jesus was not God's press agent, spin doctor, cleaning service, personal assistant, or "best boy." Jesus was God at work in the world. What Jesus does is what God is doing in the world. Yet Jesus is not all there is to God. Jesus does the Father's will and works the Father's work but is not the Father. "My Father is still working, and I also am working" (John 5:17 NRSV). Moreover, Jesus acts in the Spirit's power, yet is not the Holy Spirit. "I will ask the Father and he will give you another Advocate" (John 14:16 NRSV). Thus the doctrine of the Trinity grows out of the realization, crudely put, that Jesus is God at work in human flesh, a work God continues through the Spirit working in the church.

So the doctrine of the Trinity developed from the church's reflection on God in action. Beginning with the gospel that God's central deed is done through Jesus of Nazareth in the power of the Holy Spirit, the church recognized that divine doing has a triune pattern precisely because God has a triune identity. God does things triunely because God is triune. So, for example, the work of redeeming the world is one work accomplished by the one God who is the Father willing and the Son enacting and the Spirit perfecting it—a single divine deed with a triune pattern, a pattern that can be rendered in various ways. The early church verbalized the triune pattern through a careful use of prepositions that unite each divine person to their common work: divine doing proceeds "from the Father through the Son in the Holy Spirit."[23] What matters most is not how we word the pattern, but that we recognize it, for the full implication of Trinitarian theology is that the Triune God does all things triunely.

In addition to the pattern, there is also a triune *character* to everything God does: what God does in the world and how God does it are both intrinsically grounded in and shaped by God's identity as Father, Son, and Holy Spirit. We can see this by looking at Jesus. What he does characteristically shows us the character of divine doing. Of course, we can describe Jesus's activity as a long list of discrete actions: healing hurts, forgiving sins, restoring outcasts, loving enemies, creating community. At this level of specificity, there is no clear correspondence between what God does in the world and what God does in God's own life. There is no forgiving of sins between the Father and the Son, no healing of hurts between the Spirit and the Father, no restoring necessary between the Son and the Spirit. However, if we step back to a more inclusive description of what God is doing in Jesus, then we can begin to see the parallel, the "on earth as in heaven" pattern of divine doing. For example, we can describe all these different things that Jesus did as forms of the activity of loving (John 13:34; Rom. 5:8; Eph. 5:2). This more inclusive description makes obvious the correspondence between God's earthly and heavenly doing, for God is love (1 John 4:8, 16), and God's triune life simply is the eternal loving of the Father and the Son and the Spirit (John 3:35; 5:20; 10:17).[24] So characteristically, God's earthly action is loving precisely because it is the action of these three who are always loving one another.[25]

So both in terms of pattern and character, God acts triunely. Because in heaven the Father loves the Son in the Spirit, so on earth the Father loves us and all creation through the Son in the Spirit. We believe that everything God does has this triune pattern and character, not because we can always see it clearly, but because we see Jesus (Heb. 2:9).

God Does Father, Son, and Holy Spirit

The word *god* is a noun. So, too, are *father*, *son*, and *spirit*, and most other suggested substitutions for naming the three divine persons. We have to be careful that the grammar of our habitual speech about God doesn't mislead us into thinking that what God does can be separated from who God is. It can't. What I do can be separated from who I am, mostly. Your doing is also separable from your being, mostly. But not God's. Never. God might just as well be named by verbs as nouns. God's being, God's existence, God's life is better described as ceaseless activity than as eternal stasis. The active agency of God revealed in scripture corresponds with the activity constitutive of God's own life.

One way to get at this is to reflect on how the historical work of the Son and Spirit corresponds with their identity in the divine life. What Easter shows us is that "in Jesus, God was on a mission" to save the world.[26] Pentecost shows us that God continues the mission, now by sending the Spirit. Twice God sends God into the world to enact our salvation. We see both missional sendings in a crucial passage from Galatians:

> But when the fullness of time had come, God *sent* his Son, born of a woman, born under the law, in order to redeem those who were under the law, so that we might receive adoption as children. And because you are children, God *has sent* the Spirit of his Son into our hearts, crying "Abba! Father!" (Gal. 4:4–6 NRSV, italics mine)

The theological tradition therefore came to speak of the Father's two sendings as two missions, the Son's and the Spirit's. But it also quickly recognized that these two missions correspond to two movements within God's own life, the begetting of the Son by the Father, and the breathing forth of the Spirit by the Father through the Son.[27] To put this differently, there is a parallel between what happens in our history and what happens in God's own life. Here, the Father sends the Son and the Spirit. There, the Father "produces" the Son and the Spirit.[28]

The other way to get at the claim that God's own life is more verb than noun is by reflecting on the use of the term *person* to identify each of the Triune three. To say that the Father, Son, and Holy Spirit are persons is to use the term very differently than when we use it of Mary, Martha, and Lazarus. In our everyday usage, especially in these modern, individualist times, we think of a person as an individual whose existence precedes his or her actions, and whose personhood precedes his or her relationships. Of course there are some good reasons to critique that understanding. But even appropriately nuanced, a human person is a poor model for what we mean when we sing, "God in three persons, blessed Trinity." This is because our existence as persons is not *constantly constituted* by our relation to other persons. God's existence as three persons, on the other hand, is constantly constituted by the interrelation of these three.[29]

Let me illustrate. I was originally constituted by relation to my mother and father, and in early life they were the most formative of who I am still; even during my adolescent alienation, those relationships shaped me far more than I admitted. But those relationships were not, nor are they now, the total and ceaseless source of my very existence as a person.[30] Then I could have been orphaned without ceasing to exist. Now I can forget to call or fail to visit yet continue to be Brent. I would certainly be the poorer for it, but I would not cease to be. Moreover, I can add new relationships, and these may become more immediate and formative than those of my origin. As a husband and father (relationships that came several decades into my personhood), I now am most directly constituted by my daily relationship with my wife and children. So with me relationships may come and go, may wax or wane, but they are not my personhood itself; they are not the constant source or sustaining power of my very existence as a person.

It is otherwise with God. The three divine persons are always and only because of their relationship to one another.[31] Or to say that in terms of divine doing, the three divine persons exist because of and in and through their ceaseless activity of relating. The Son is because of the Father's begetting. The Nicene Creed affirms that this begetting is eternal, implying not just that it occurs outside the created flow of time, but that the Son always is because the Father always begets. Now hypothetically, if that begetting came to an end, the Son would too, and so would the Father.[32] That's what it means to be constantly constituted by relationship. One's very existence, one's "to be," is a matter of the ceaseless activity of relating. While trinitarian theology has a whole range of technical terminology to characterize these inter-relations, we can step back and say more generally that the three divine persons are persons because of their ceaseless giving to and receiving from one another.[33] God's being as three persons is an unceasing giving and receiving, an ongoing divine activity, what God is always doing.

Thomas Weinandy's way of putting all this is that "the terms 'Father,' 'Son,' and 'Holy Spirit' are therefore *verbs*, for they refer to, define, and name, solely and exclusively, the *interrelated acts* by which all three persons are who they are."[34] My way is more terse, but I think makes the identical point: God does Father, Son, and Holy Spirit.

Practicing Trinity

So what? Even if we can, rightly nuanced and carefully articu-lated, affirm that "God does Father, Son, and Holy Spirit," why should we care? What significance might that have for Christian discipleship? As Jason Byassee argued earlier in this book, we are created to desire and delight in God. That alone provides sufficient reason for an extended reflection on and contemplation of the intrinsic relation between who God is and what God does.

But given the myriad distortions in popular culture attached to proclamations that God did this or God will do that, it seem particularly prudent to conclude with four brief reflections on why it matters that God does Father, Son, and Holy Spirit. In doing so, I am following the claims of David Cunningham, Colin Gunton, and others that the Trinity is actually a doctrine that Christians can practice.[35]

First, we practice the doctrine of the Trinity when we baptize in the name of the Father and the Son and the Holy Spirit. Baptism in the Triune name can be considered the core trinitarian practice of the church. But as practiced and understood, it too easily overlooks the intrinsic connection between God's doing and ours. That happens when the triune formula is taken merely as an identification of which God the baptizand is now identified with. Christian baptism claims you for the Father, Son, and Holy Spirit rather than for Vishnu or Rah; it identifies you with the Triune God rather than Elvis or elves. All true, but not the whole truth.

Baptism isn't just about identification; it is also about incorporation. The action of baptism incorporates us into the saving action of the Father through the Son in the Spirit. And because God's action in the world corresponds to God's internal, eternal activity of giving and receiving, what baptism does is include us in a ceaseless cycle of receiving all that we are as gift and offering it back as grateful response. "God does Father, Son, and Holy Spirit" might just suggest to us that baptism inaugurates a life of doing that corresponds to what is done in God's own triune life.

This leads to the second answer to "So what?"—worship. Trinitarian doxologies have been a common feature of the gathered worship of the people of God, but too often they had been taken as a cognitive claim about God that bears little relation to the actual structure of our worship itself. James Torrance characterizes this as a "unitarian" understanding of worship, one in which God sits over there waiting to receive our worship and we stand over here trying to heave it across the gap that separates us.[36] Such a popular understanding of worship sees it as something we do to or for God, who may have done something to elicit our worship and may even do something in response, but who does nothing *in* our worship but passively receive our praise.

Contrast that with a trinitarian understanding of the shape of worship, one that recognizes that just as God's creating and redeeming work is from the Father through the Son in the Spirit, so our responsive return of praise runs to the Father through the Son in the Spirit.[37] In worship we are not commanded to "do something" worthy of God, but rather are invited to enter fully into what is already being done—the ongoing sacrifice of the Son to the Father in the Spirit. So Trinitarian worship is not merely an affirmation of the self-offering of Jesus, or even an imitation of it, but is a participation in that offering, a communion in the Son's active response to the Father. Saying "God does Father, Son, and Holy Spirit" once in a while might just remind us that in worship we are entering into what the Triune God is doing.

Third, "God does Father, Son, and Holy Spirit" implies that the diversity or plurality of God's own identity is not something God suffers or endures. Think about how shifting from the verb of being (*is*) to an active verb like *does* implies a certain intentionality on God's part. That is actually one of the dangers of my formulation, because it could suggest to us that God woke up one morning and decided to start doing the Trinity, or that someday God might get tired of doing Trinity and do something different, or that God has desires and wants like the rest of us. Those inferences are silly. But because these three persons are constituted by their own ceaseless activity of giving and receiving, we can infer that God freely wills to be who God is—that the differentiation and plurality that constitute God's own inner life is precisely who God "wants to be."

It is therefore in character that God graciously opens the divine life to participation by that which is not God. Of course, creation is a different act, and so is redemption. But both acts nonetheless correspond to the free welcome of difference and reception of otherness that already constitute God's own life. No wonder, then, that Jesus brings together "a great multitude . . . from every nation, from all tribes and peoples and languages" (Rev. 7:9 NRSV). Therefore, to say that "God does Father, Son, and Holy Spirit" ought to remind us that hospitality to difference is at the very heart of God's own life and thus must govern the church's life together.

Finally, remembering that "God does Father, Son, and Holy Spirit" might help us live more faithfully in a world where people are prone to say things like, "God brought Katrina to punish America," or "God gave me a promotion because I really honored him," or "God wants to write your love story," or "God will cure your cancer if you really believe," or "God always requires blood to make things right," or "God doesn't hurry, but he sure ought to," or "God costars in my life movie." In the face of such careless speech and sloppy thinking, we might begin to want an explanation of why God allows suffering and sin and death, or a theory of how God acts in and for the world. But we shouldn't be anxious, for God does not leave us speechless. Instead, the Father offers us the Word eternally uttered and the Spirit ever witnessing; that is, God offers us a participation in the divine doing that is God's eternal communion. So we don't finally know why there are tsunamis in God's good creation, nor how God does a deed like resurrection, but we do know God, the God who is—and does—Father, Son, and Holy Spirit.

Notes

Introduction: God Does All Things Well

1. "Hero Assam: God helped me shoot gunman Matthew Murray," *Melbourne Herald Sun*, December 12, 2007 (accessed online February 29, 2008).

2. CNN story of December 10, 2007, accessed at http://www.cnn.com/2007/US/12/10/colorado.shootings/index.html on February 29, 2008.

3. Ibid.

4. Fox News story of December 11, 2007, "Guard Who Shot Colorado Gunman: God Helped Me," accessed at http://www.foxnews.com/story/0,2933,316419,00.html on February 29, 2008.

Chapter 1 God Does Not Wear a White Coat—but God Does Heal

1. For a good theological discussion of this phenomenon see Ingolf Dalferth, "'I Determine What God Is!': Theology in an Age of 'Cafeteria Religion,'" *Theology Today* 57, no. 1 (2000): 5–23.

2. Herbert Benson, *Beyond the Relaxation Response* (New York: Berkley, 1984), 81–82, emphasis original.

3. For more on these matters, see Joel Shuman, *The Body of Compassion* (Boulder: Westview, 1999), 142–56; and Joel Shuman and Keith Meador, *Heal Thyself: Spirituality, Medicine, and the Distortion of Christianity* (New York: Oxford, 2003), 123–26.

4. Wendell Berry, "Health Is Membership," in *Another Turn of the Crank* (Washington, DC: Counterpoint, 1995), 90.

5. See Genesis 12:1–5; 15:1–6; 22:15–19; 28:10–22.

6. Hence, the prohibition in the Decalogue against making improper use of God's name. For more on this, see D. Brent Laytham, ed., *God Is Not* (Grand Rapids: Brazos, 2004), 122–28.

7. For more on this point, see Gerhard Von Rad, *Old Testament Theology,* vol. 1: *The Theology of Israel's Historical Traditions,* trans. D. M. G. Stalker (Edinburgh: Oliver and Boyd, 1962), 179–87.

8. Luke adds in his Gospel a detail that makes Jesus seem even wilder; he heals the severed ear as he reproves the sword-wielding disciple.

9. Here see John Howard Yoder, *The Politics of Jesus* (Grand Rapids: Eerdmans, 1972).

10. The author of Hebrews (12:2) maintains that in accepting the cross Jesus becomes the "pioneer and perfecter" of faith.

11. Here see 1 Cor. 2:1–3:23; 12:22–26 and 2 Cor. 11:30–12:10.

12. See Joel Shuman and Brian Volck, *Reclaiming the Body: Christians and the Faithful Use of Modern Medicine* (Grand Rapids: Brazos, 2006), 27–40.

13. The best statement of this position is found in Yoder, *The Politics of Jesus.*

14. On this point see Berry, "Health Is Membership," 83–109.

15. John Howard Yoder, "A People in the World," in *The Royal Priesthood,* ed. Michael Cartwright (Grand Rapids: Eerdmans, 1994), 74.

Chapter 2 God Does Not Demand Blood

1. Jonathan Edwards, "Sinners in the Hands of an Angry God," in *The Works of Jonathan Edwards,* vol. 2, ed. Edward Hickman (Carlisle, PA: Banner of Truth Trust, 1974), 9.

2. J. Daryl Charles, *Between Pacifism and Jihad* (Downers Grove, IL: InterVarsity, 2005), 111.

3. Dave Grossman, *On Killing* (Boston: Little, Brown, 1995).

4. See, for example, Martin Luther King Jr., "An Experiment in Love," in *A Testament of Hope,* ed. James M. Washington, (San Francisco: HarperCollins, 1991), 9.

5. For a more extensive treatment of Anselm, see Daniel M. Bell Jr., "Forgiveness and the End of Economy," *Studies in Christian Ethics* 20, no. 3 (2007): 325–44.

6. For this reading of Romans, see Luke Timothy Johnson, *Rereading Romans* (Macon, GA: Smyth & Helwys, 2001); and A. Katherine Grieb, *The Story of Romans* (Louisville: Westminster John Knox, 2002). For more on God's justice in Romans and the tradition more broadly, see Daniel M. Bell Jr., "Jesus, the Jews, and the Politics of God's Justice," *Ex Auditu* 22 (2006): 87–112.

7. This is a particularly important distinction in light of situations of domestic violence. What I have said is not an exhortation to victims to remain in violent situations. We are not called merely to bear violence—passively enduring violence. We are called to be prepared to bear violence in order to bear it away. One who is in a situation of domestic violence is not in a position to bear violence in order to bear it away. Thus, victims should get help and get out. Bearing violence in order to bear it away may come later, as the response of a community that is prepared to risk loving perpetrators—bearing them and the burden of their vice—in the hope of redeeming them, bearing that violence away. In other

words, one is a deliberate, disciplined communal practice that seeks to eliminate the violence; the other is an isolated suffering with no end in sight.

8. See Daniel M. Bell Jr., "Just War as Christian Discipleship," Ekklesia Project Renewing Radical Discipleship pamphlet series #14.

9. See Christopher Marshall, *Beyond Retribution: A New Testament Vision for Justice, Crime, and Punishment* (Grand Rapids: Eerdmans, 2001); Howard Zehr *Changing Lenses: A New Focus on Crime and Justice* (Scottdale, PA: Herald Press, 1990); Daniel M. Bell Jr., "Justice and Liberation," in *The Blackwell Companion to Christian Ethics,* eds. Stanley Hauerwas and Sam Wells (Malden, MA: Blackwell, 2003), 182–95.

10. Ezek. 18:32 NRSV.

Chapter 3 God Does Not Hurry

1. Andrew Lam, "Stress (or "Si-Tress") Vietnamese Style," Oct. 12, 2006, accessed at http://blogs.newamericamedia.org/andrew-lam/281/stress-vietnamese-style-an-npr-commentary on May 31, 2007.

2. See Eric Schlosser's fascinating *Fast Food Nation: The Dark Side of an All-American Meal* (New York: HarperCollins, 2002).

3. A fascinating example, relative to this essay, is Stephen M. R. Covey, *The Speed of Trust: The One Thing that Changes Everything* (New York: Free Press, 2006). Covey argues that corporations need to cultivate trusting relations to streamline their decision making.

4. I began noticing this phrase in the late 1990s. It seems to capture a sort of despair about setting the past right and an eagerness to cast nostalgia as the enemy. I think of it as related to the less formal "Bygones."

5. The earliest use I've found of the term "burned out" is in an essay by Charles F. Warnath and John L. Shelton, "The Ultimate Disappointment: The Burned-Out Counselor," *Personnel and Guidance Journal*, December 1976: 172–75. At any rate, the term became common in the 1970s.

6. Gerhard Lohfink, *Does God Need the Church? Toward a Theology of the People of God,* trans. Linda M. Maloney (Collegeville, MN: Liturgical Press, 1999), 26.

7. Ibid., 27.

8. I cite this from David Bailey Harned, *Patience: How We Wait upon the World* (Cambridge, MA: Cowley, 1997), 28, who credits the quote to Barth from *Church Dogmatics* II/1, 413. My comments on humility and trust are much indebted to Harned.

9. See Marva Dawn, *A Royal "Waste" of Time: The Splendor of Worshiping God and Being Church for the World* (Grand Rapids: Eerdmans, 1999).

10. David Landes, "Of Time: Work, Prayer, and Monks," in *On Moral Business: Classical and Contemporary Resources for Ethics in Economic Life,* ed. Max L. Stackhouse, Dennis P. McCann, and Shirley J. Roels, with Preston N. Williams (Grand Rapids: Eerdmans, 1995), 253–58.

11. The many writings of Jean Vanier, such as *Befriending the Stranger* (Grand Rapids: Eerdmans, 2006) and the now classic *Community and Growth* (Mahwah, NJ: Paulist Press, 1989), are rich aids to anyone interested in growing in patience and trust.

12. Accessed at http://www.stanford.edu/group/King/frequentdocs/clergy .pdf, May 31, 2007.

13. Accessed at http://www.thekingcenter.org/prog/non/Letter.pdf, May 31, 2007.

14. Accessed at http://www.zenit.org/english/visualizza.phtml?sid=86756, May 31, 2007.

15. J.R.R. Tolkien, *The Silmarillion* (London: George Allen & Unwin, 1977), 15.

16. Ibid., 16.

17. Ibid., 17.

18. I owe thanks to Ethan Smith and Nikki Coffey Tousley for their assistance in the research and shaping of this chapter, as well as to the participants in the 2006 Monastic Institute at St. John's University, Collegeville, whose witness taught me much about patience.

Chapter 4 God Does Not Want to Write Your Love Story

1. Eric and Leslie Ludy, *When God Writes Your Love Story: The Ultimate Approach to Guy/Girl Relationships* (Sisters, OR: Loyal Publishing, 1999); cf. also, inter alia, Leslie Ludy, *Authentic Beauty: The Shaping of a Set-Apart Young Woman* (Sisters, OR: Multnomah, 2003); Joshua Harris, *I Kissed Dating Goodbye: A New Attitude toward Romance and Relationships* (Sisters, OR: Multnomah, 1997) and *Boy Meets Girl: Say Hello to Courtship* (Sisters, OR: Multnomah, 2000); John Eldredge, *Wild at Heart: Discovering the Secret of a Man's Soul* (Nashville: Thomas Nelson, 2006) and *Captivating: Unveiling the Mystery of a Woman's Soul* (Nashville: Thomas Nelson, 2005); Heather Arnel Paulsen, *Emotional Purity: An Affair of the Heart* (Wheaton: Crossway, 2007).

2. Laura Sessions Stepp, *Unhooked: How Young Women Pursue Sex, Delay Love and Lose at Both* (New York: Riverhead, 2007).

3. Timothy Egan, "Erotica Inc.," *New York Times*, October 23, 2000.

4. Leslie Ludy, in *When God Writes Your Love Story*, 224.

5. Ibid., 129.

6. Jesus, lover of my soul, let me to Thy bosom fly,
While the nearer waters roll, while the tempest still is high.
Hide me, O my Savior, hide, till the storm of life is past;
Safe into the haven guide; O receive my soul at last.

Other refuge have I none, hangs my helpless soul on Thee;
Leave, ah! leave me not alone, still support and comfort me.
All my trust on Thee is stayed, all my help from Thee I bring;
Cover my defenseless head with the shadow of Thy wing.

Wilt Thou not regard my call? Wilt Thou not accept my prayer?
Lo! I sink, I faint, I fall—Lo! on Thee I cast my care;
Reach me out Thy gracious hand! While I of Thy strength receive,
Hoping against hope I stand, dying, and behold, I live.

Thou, O Christ, art all I want, more than all in Thee I find;
Raise the fallen, cheer the faint, heal the sick, and lead the blind.
Just and holy is Thy Name, I am all unrighteousness;
False and full of sin I am; Thou art full of truth and grace.

Plenteous grace with Thee is found, grace to cover all my sin;
Let the healing streams abound; make and keep me pure within.
Thou of life the fountain art, freely let me take of Thee;
Spring Thou up within my heart; rise to all eternity.

Chapter 5 God Does Not Entertain

1. Dietrich Bonhoeffer: *London, 1933–1935*, vol. 13 of *Works* (Minneapolis: Fortress, 2007), 323.

2. From *The Desert Fathers: Sayings of the Early Christian Monks,* trans. Benedicta Ward (London: Penguin, 2003), 10.

3. *Christianity Today's* is one of the best and most popular: www.christianity today.com/movies. The United States Conference of Catholic Bishops grades films on mostly pious grounds: http://www.usccb.org/movies/.

4. A few of the better ones: Robert Johnston, *Reel Spirituality: Theology and Film in Dialogue*, 2nd ed. (Grand Rapids: Baker, 2006); Greg Garrett, *The Gospel According to Hollywood* (Louisville: Westminster, 2007); Roy Anker, *Catching Light: Looking for God in the Movies* (Grand Rapids: Eerdmans, 2004); Craig Detweiler and Barry Taylor, *A Matrix of Meanings: Finding God in Pop Culture* (Grand Rapids: Baker, 2003).

5. Quoted in Johnston, *Reel Spirituality,* 22. Teaching a course on theology and film at Northern Baptist Theological Seminary in the fall of 2007, I found my students returning to this quote repeatedly as the best argument for engaging popular culture theologically. I am grateful to them for helping me think through these issues, and especially to Jason Morriss for his critical comments on an earlier draft of this essay.

6. "A Review of the Passion," at www.bibleinterp.com.

7. *Nickel and Dimed: On (Not) Getting By in America* (New York: Holt, 2002).

8. See Leonid Ouspensky and Vladimir Lossky, *The Meaning of Icons* (Crestwood, NY: St. Vladimir's Press, 1983). For the arguments made firsthand, see St. John of Damascus, *On the Divine Images,* trans. David Anderson (Crestwood: St. Vladimir's Press, 1997).

9. Johnston, *Reel Spirituality*, 38.

10. See his wonderful essay "Incarnation," in *Pro Ecclesia*, vol. 2, no. 2 (1993): 208–215.

11. Garrett, *The Gospel According to Hollywood* (Louisville: Westminster, 2007).

12. For a characteristically sophisticated and elegant working out of this criticism of incarnational theology, especially in Anglican circles, see Rowan Williams' "Incarnation and the Renewal of Community" in *On Christian Theology* (Oxford: Blackwell, 2000), 225–38.

13. Debra Dean Murphy makes this argument categorically against PowerPoint in worship in her "PowerPointless," *Christian Century*, July 25, 2006, 10.

14. St. Augustine, *Confessions*, translated by Henry Chadwick (New York: Oxford University Press, 1991), 137.

15. A good defense of natural law remains C. S. Lewis's *The Abolition of Man* (New York: Simon & Schuster, 1996).

16. Barth's exposition of secular parables, or lesser lights alongside the greater Light, comes in his *Church Dogmatics* IV/3.1, *The Doctrine of Reconciliation*, trans. G.W. Bromiley and T. F. Torrance (Edinburgh: T & T Clark, 1961).

17. Kevin Vanhoozer has an appropriately underdetermined philosophical account of the presence of truth in secular culture. Rather than give a general theory of this phenomenon, Vanhoozer suggests Christians "poach" on culture, scavenging what works, laying claim to what's rightfully theirs when its owner isn't looking. See his book with Charles Anderson and Michael Sleasman, *Everybody Theology: How to Read Cultural Texts and Interpret Trends* (Grand Rapids: Baker, 2007).

18. This is a practice I very much wish to discourage. Perhaps it comes from personal experience: it was innovative when my youth pastor showed us clips from *The Wonder Years* when I was in high school. But what do I remember of it? That my cool pastor showed us clips from *The Wonder Years*. Nothing about the "moral to the story," nothing about Jesus or my neighbor. Just that it was cool. I suspect this is what most worship-attenders remember when they have movie clips inflicted on them. Eventually, they'll just stay home or go to the cineplex. Why go to church to get what you expect someplace else?

19. These quotes come from *Quodvultdeus of Carthage: The Creedal Homilies*, trans. Thomas Finn (New York: Newman Press, 2004), 25.

20. I echo here my article "Jedi or Jesuit?" in *Books and Culture*, May/June 2005.

Chapter 6 God Does Father, Son, and Holy Spirit

1. The phrase "lets be" is not intended to undercut the claim that God brings it into existence, but only to catch the nuance of blessed permission in the Genesis 1 phrasing "let there be," to hear there God freeing rather than forcing existence out of nothing. On this, note Walter Brueggemann's claim that that at creation God's "sovereign speech is not coercive but evocative. It invites but does not compel" (*Genesis* [Atlanta: Westminster John Knox Press, 1982], 18).

2. Colin Gunton connects pneumatology and eschatology with the claim that "God the Spirit is the mediator of God's eschatological action *over against and toward* the order of his creation" (emphasis original) (*The Christian Faith: An Introduction to Christian Doctrine* [Malden, MA: Blackwell, 2002], 111).

3. See the discussion by Gregory of Nyssa in William G. Rusch, ed. and trans., *The Trinitarian Controversy* (Minneapolis: Fortress, 1980), 155–57.

4. This claim about the unity of God's action does not mean that we cannot differentiate how the persons work or discern differing emphases. That is the

very thing I've done above by saying it is the consistent work of the Holy Spirit to bring to perfection all that God does.

5. Miroslav Volf uses "giving and forgiving" to characterize creation and redemption in his marvelous book *Free of Charge: Giving and Forgiving in a Culture Stripped of Grace* (Grand Rapids: Zondervan, 2005).

6. "God's action in and towards the world takes the form of *both* creating what is *and* redeeming what has failed to become what it is called to be" (Colin Gunton, *Father, Son and Holy Spirit* [New York: T&T Clark, 2003], 137).

7. Catherine Mowry LaCugna, "God in Communion with Us—The Trinity," in LaCugna, ed., *Freeing Theology: The Essentials of Theology in Feminist Perspective* (San Francisco: HarperCollins, 1993), 100. David Cunningham notes, "When we use words that have a great many 'male' associations (and in the case of *father* and *son,* these associations are almost exclusively male), it seems likely that these associations will be carried over to the reality to which the word is attempting to refer" (Cunningham, *These Three Are One* [Malden, MA: Blackwell, 1998], 50).

8. One way of critiquing this strategy of attaching ourselves to divine activity with "co-" is to point to the analogical character of the verbs *create* and *redeem* when they are used of God's action. They do not literally mean the same thing of God's doing as they do of ours, and slapping "co-" on the front of *creator* simply rushes past that massive distinction. For a theological critique of *co-creator* as undercutting creation *ex nihilo,* see Stanley Hauerwas, "Work as Co-Creation: A Critique of a Remarkably Bad Idea," chapter 7 of *In Good Company* (Notre Dame: University of Notre Dame Press, 1995); see especially 111–14.

9. For a nuanced discussion of such distinctions, see Miroslav Volf's exposition of how our giving is both like and unlike God's in *Free of Charge,* 61–63.

10. This claim is "ontological" rather than "epistemological." That means it is a claim about what really is the case, but not necessarily about how we come to know it. In the order of knowing, first Israel discovers through God's steadfast covenant love that God is Father in relation to Israel, and indeed in relation to the whole world. But in the order of being, in terms of what has eternally been the case, God is Father of God the Son.

11. Just as *teacher* cannot avoid implying teaching (the activity) and students (the activity's object), so *Creator, Redeemer,* and *Sustainer* each imply an active relation between agent (God) and object (the world, or some portion of it).

12. Note that if we take the words bare, neither *Son* nor *Spirit* immediately implies a specific God–world relationship, and, as we've already acknowledged, the relation that *Father* suggests is fraught with false inferences of a gendered deity and a patriarchal providence.

13. See Lawrence Porter, OP, "On Keeping 'Persons' in the Trinity: A Linguistic Approach to Trinitarian Thought," *Theological Studies* 41 (S 1980): 530–48; 542. As LaCugna puts it, the Christian doctrine of the Trinity means that God "is essentially and necessarily personal" (LaCugna, "God in Communion with Us," in LaCugna, ed., *Freeing Theology,* 105; emphasis original).

14. I put it precisely this way because some readers will be aware of the historical claim that Marcion's refusal of the OT and severe editing of Paul and Luke was the impetus for the church to develop its own, competing canon. Against

this construal, John Barton has argued fairly convincingly that the church's canon was fairly well developed (or developing) before Marcion arrived on the scene, and that it was (as Irenaeus and other antiheretical writers argued) precisely because of this already existing sense of a biblical whole that the church was able to say no to Marcion.

15. Quoted by J. A. DiNoia, OP, "Knowing and Naming the Triune God: The Grammar of Trinitarian Confession," in Alvin F. Kimel, ed., *Speaking the Christian God* (Grand Rapids: Eerdmans, 1992), 162. DiNoia expounds Catherine's words thus: "As Christians have understood it, to affirm the presence of God's 'very self' in grace is to affirm the personal presence of the Blessed Trinity" (162).

16. I'm implying here that both Arianism and subordinationism in general make the mistake of dividing trinitarian action, with the result that only the Creator is truly God and the other persons become the object of divine doing rather than the subject.

17. Walter Brueggemann, *Theology of the Old Testament* (Minneapolis: Fortress, 1997), 123. Subsequent references are made parenthetically in this paragraph.

18. John 3:34 notes the agency of the Holy Spirit in God's speaking. Acts 10:38 notes the agency of the Holy Spirit in God's reconciling work in Jesus. John 4 connects the Spirit with God's loving and giving. Romans 1:4, 8:11, and 1 Peter 3:18 hint at the agency of the Holy Spirit in God's raising Jesus from the dead.

19. The quote and the sentiment are from Langdon B. Gilkey's classic refusal of the claim that God acts, in "Cosmology, Ontology, and the Travail of Biblical Language," first published in *Journal of Religion*, 1961, and quoted in William C. Placher, *Domestication of Transcendence* (Louisville: Westminster John Knox Press, 1996), 190. Gilkey goes on to say, "To us, theological verbs such as 'to act,' 'to work,' 'to do,' 'to speak,' 'to reveal,' etc., have no longer the literal meaning of observable actions in space and time or of voices in the air." The interesting question is when these theological verbs had a literal meaning. The theological tradition has long understood the analogical character of these verbs. Certainly, naive biblical literalism has always existed, but it has not necessarily been as widespread as modern contempt for our rustic forebears thinks. Indeed, the real problem of literalism emerges with and because of the modernist intellectual outlook Gilkey espouses.

20. Robert W. Jenson, *Systematic Theology,* vol. 1 (New York: Oxford University Press, 1997), 4.

21. Placher, *Domestication of Transcendence,* 195. That is certainly what Paul seems to do in his longest treatment of resurrection (1 Cor. 15).

22. David Cunningham, "What Do We Mean by 'God'?" in William Placher, ed., *Essentials of Christian Theology* (Louisville: Westminster, 2003), 77.

23. See Geoffrey Wainwright, "Trinitarian Worship," in Kimel, ed., *Speaking the Christian God,* 210. And the pattern can also be indicated, though not as clearly, by the use of conjunctions: divine doing is by the Father *and* the Son *together with* the Holy Spirit.

24. Of course, the theological tradition has various ways of articulating this divine loving. Augustine, for example, speaks of the Father as the Lover, the Son as the Beloved, and the Holy Spirit as the love that binds them together.

25. Similarly, Miroslav Volf characterizes God's activity as giving in *Free of Charge*. In God's inner life, "divine persons exchange gifts—the gift of themselves and the gift of the others glory" (85). In God's relation to creation, God is the unceasing giver.

26. ". . . in Jesus, God was on a mission . . ." (Cunningham in Placher, *Domestication of Transcedence*, 78).

27. In technical theology, these two movements are called "processions," as both the Son and the Spirit are somehow a going-out from the Father. One of the thorniest issues in the divided Christian church is whether the Holy Spirit proceeds only from the Father or proceeds from the Father *and the Son* (in Latin *filioque*). This controversy continues to divide the Eastern and Western church and cannot be settled here.

28. I borrow "produce" from Nicholas Lash in *Believing Three Ways in One God* (Notre Dame: University of Notre Dame Press, 1993).

29. See the discussion of this by Thomas Weinandy, *Does God Suffer?* (Notre Dame: University of Notre Dame Press, 2000), 114n19. I am using the phrase "constantly constituted by" to express what Thomas Aquinas means by the term "subsistent relation."

30. The one exception to this is the period of gestation in the womb, an interrelation David Cunningham uses effectively as an analogy for the Triune relations.

31. "The Father, the Son and the Holy Spirit solely and completely are who they are only in relation to one another." Weinandy, *Does God Suffer?*, 118.

32. "The Father subsists eternally as Father only in relation to the Son and to the Holy Spirit, for his very identity as Father is predicated upon his being the origin of the Son and of the Holy Spirit, and so he is constituted as Father in the one eternal act of begetting the Son and spirating the Holy Spirit. The Father then only subsists as Father in and by giving himself wholly as Father in the begetting of his Son. He gives himself wholly in the begetting of the Son through the Holy Spirit. The Father then equally and simultaneously gives himself wholly in spirating the Holy Spirit for the Holy Spirit proceeds from the Father as the fullness of his fatherly love in and by whom the Father begets the Son. Thus, the Son and the Holy Spirit are fully divine only because the Father has given himself wholly as Father, and the Father is Father only because his whole identity is founded upon the action of his complete giving of himself" (Weinandy, *Does God Suffer?*, 116–17). In some sense, this passage is the heart of my entire argument in this chapter.

33. "The point about the communion that is the Trinity is that in God the three persons are such that they receive from and give to each other their unique particularity. They have their being in relation to one another. The Son is not the Father, but receives his being from him; the Father cannot be the Father without the Son; and so on" (Gunton, *Father, Son and Holy Spirit*, 16).

34. Weinandy, *Does God Suffer?*, 118 (italics original).

35. "The Church has failed to practice the Trinity" (Gunton, *The Christian Faith*, 18).

36. James B. Torrance, *Worship, Community and the Triune God of Grace* (Downers Grove, IL: InterVarsity, 1996), chapter 1.

37. In worship there is dialogue between God and humanity, a movement from God to humanity, and a responsive movement from humanity to God. The first is "a God-humanward movement, from (*ek*) the Father, through (*dia*) the Son, in (*en*) the Spirit," and in the second "a human-Godward movement to the Father, through the Son in the Spirit" (Torrance, *Worship, Community and the Triune God of Grace*, 32).